ME AND
SISTER BOBBIE

ME AND SISTER BOBBIE

TRUE TALES OF THE FAMILY BAND

WILLIE NELSON AND BOBBIE NELSON

WITH DAVID RITZ

RANDOM HOUSE
NEW YORK

Published in the United States by Random House, an imprint and
division of Penguin Random House LLC, New York.

RANDOM HOUSE and the HOUSE colophon are registered trademarks
of Penguin Random House LLC.

Library of Congress Cataloging-in-Publication Data
Names: Nelson, Willie, 1933– author. | Nelson, Bobbie, author. |
Ritz, David, author.
Title: Me and sister Bobbie: true tales of the family band / Willie Nelson
and Bobbie Nelson; with David Ritz.
Description: First edition. | New York: Random House, 2020.
Identifiers: LCCN 2020005622 (print) | LCCN 2020005623 (ebook) |
ISBN 9781984854131 (hardcover) | ISBN 9781984854148 (ebook)
Subjects: LCSH: Nelson, Willie, 1933– | Nelson, Bobbie. |
Country musicians—United States—Biography.
Classification: LCC ML420.N4 A3 2020 (print) | LCC ML420.N4 (ebook) |
DDC 782.421642092/2 [B]—dc23
LC record available at https://lccn.loc.gov/2020005622
LC ebook record available at https://lccn.loc.gov/2020005623

Printed in the United States of America on acid-free paper

randomhousebooks.com

2 4 6 8 9 7 5 3 1

First Edition

For Mama and Daddy Nelson

PART I

THE STORY BEGINS . . .

BROTHER

Nearly nine decades. A long lifetime.

Hard to believe that it was sixty years ago I wrote a song called "Funny How Time Slips Away." Wrote it when I was only twenty-seven, and I really didn't know what I was talking about. Except I did. As a kid, I was only imagining a romance that had gone sour. As it turned out, my imagination was pretty good. Little did I know that one day I'd wake up and realize I have enough memories to fill a shelf of books. I've written a few books before, but there's one that passed me by. Probably passed me by 'cause the heroine is too humble to demand attention. The heroine is my sister, Bobbie.

Bobbie's got the best story in our whole family. But to tell it right, I needed Bobbie by my side. I needed Bobbie to tell it herself. It's our good fortune that Bobbie has agreed. Without my sister, I'd never be where I am today. I've always needed her.

I was born restless. Born curious. Born ready to run. And I did. Started running at an early age. Kept running, stumbling, getting back up and running some more. Would have run into complete ruin if it hadn't been for my first and best friend, Bobbie. If I was the sky, Bobbie was the earth. She grounded me. Two years older, she also protected me.

She was there at the very beginning and remains with me,

on- and offstage, to this very day. There's no stronger or longer or steadier relationship in my life. Our stories are intertwined as only sibling stories can be. Many a time she's mended my broken heart. Many a time I've tried to mend hers. In the Nelson family, high drama comes with the territory. Crazy twists and turns began in our childhood and never stopped. Good breaks and bad breaks, triumphs and tragedies.

My bond with Bobbie is a testimony to the healing power of family. Ironically, perhaps, our bond was born out of the collapse of our original family. It could have been devastating, except I was a toddler when it happened. I have no memory of the actual event.

But for Bobbie, it was different.

SISTER

Willie and I had always lived with Dad's parents, Alfred and Nancy Nelson. I was not told why. I liked the arrangement because our grandparents were kind and caring. But I was also comforted by the knowledge that my mom and dad lived right next to us. Willie and I saw them every day. My parents rounded out my world. So to see that world fall apart scared me to death.

I was a little girl when my grandparents told me that my mother and father were leaving Abbott, the little Texas town where Willie and I were born. Not only were they leaving us, they were leaving each other. My father had another woman. None of this made sense to me. It just brought on a torrent of fear.

It happened in a flash. There was no preparation. I remember seeing two cars parked outside my grandparents' house. My mother came in to kiss me goodbye. My dad did the same. All they said was that they were going away. That's it. Then they were gone.

I was three years old.

I didn't know about "going away." No one "went away" in our world. We all stayed in Abbott.

A woman named Lorraine was waiting in my father's car.

He was going away with her. My mother was going away in another car.

I was hysterical, screaming and crying my little eyes out. I held on to my father's shirt, held on to my mother's blouse, held on to both of them so tightly that my grandfather had to drag me away screaming.

He took me to the bedroom I shared with Willie, closed the door, and locked it. The click of the lock was a dagger through my heart. I sobbed until I couldn't breathe. It didn't seem right. It wasn't fair. I had no say-so in the matter. How could that be?

I wept for hours. It felt like life was over.

No mother, no father. It can't happen just like that.

I can't remember the words they said. I'm sure they tried to explain, but none of the words mattered. What mattered was that they were leaving, and I knew that nothing would ever be the same.

Willie, only six months old, had been crawling around the house. When he saw me crying, he stopped. He was a happy spirit, but he sensed my panic. He looked at me with worry in his eyes. He'd never seen me break down before, not like this. I picked him up and held him in my arms.

"Don't worry, little brother," I said.

He knew only a few words like "mama" and "dada."

Now he said something I hadn't heard before.

"Sister," he said, though it sounded like *itta.* As he spoke, he smiled. His smile got to me. I was able to stop crying.

BROTHER

We were isolated. I know that now, but I didn't know it then.

Abbott, population four hundred, is a tiny farm community in Hill County halfway between Dallas and Waco. Bobbie was born January 1, 1931, and I made my appearance April 29, 1933. We were babies of the Great Depression. My father's folks had come to Texas from Arkansas. One of their daughters, Clara, had died young, and their other daughter, Rosa, had moved to Aquilla, close to Abbott. My grandparents, always wanting to be close to their children and grandchildren, followed Rosa to Texas.

My dad, Ira, was a car mechanic. He was also a fiddler and guitarist who played in barrooms on the county line where drinking was legal. Texas was funny like that. In certain counties, booze couldn't be served, but in other counties it could. Our dad liked to drink. In my growing-up days, most of the men were drinkers. That was normal. Also seemed to be what it meant to be a man. Dad's drinking never got in the way of my loving him. He was a great guy who just wasn't ready to be a parent. He and Mom married when they were sixteen. His folks saw that the young couple couldn't properly take care of Bobbie and me. That's why my grandparents took us in.

For as long as I can remember, Bobbie and I called them Mama and Daddy Nelson. They anchored us, raised us, and kept us—or at least tried to keep me—on the straight and narrow. They never said a bad word about our mother and father, but I knew that Mama and Daddy Nelson didn't approve of their son's drinking. He loved his parents, but he loved his whiskey and he was gonna live his life the way he wanted to. My grandparents didn't hide their feelings—they warned me about the dangers of drinking—but they also never tried to keep my father away from me or Bobbie. When he moved to Covington, only twenty-five miles from Abbott, he remained part of our lives. Every time he showed up in Abbott, tipsy or sober, we were happy to see him. Our mother went off in a different direction.

SISTER

I believe my brother's happy-go-lucky personality stayed happy-go-lucky because he wasn't traumatized by the shock of our parents' departure. He was too young to understand what was going on. But the trauma got to me.

Unlike our father, our mother didn't remain anywhere even remotely close by. As a girl, I was deeply affected. All girls crave their mother's company. Making the abandonment even more painful was the fact that my mom, Myrle Greenhaw, was an amazing woman. The sound of her sad but sweet singing voice has never left me.

Mother was of Native American heritage, three-quarters Cherokee. Strikingly beautiful, she was also a modern woman. She carried a miniature talisman of the Buddha in her purse. She wore pants, bobbed her hair, dealt cards, loved dancing, and smoked cigarettes—all things Abbott women of that era were not supposed to do. She was fiercely independent. Texans looked at her as a Mexican, and when she moved to Oklahoma she was seen as an Indian. In Abbott, she was scorned for her ethnic appearance.

All this I learned from Mildred, our cousin who lived with us. Mildred was twelve years older than me and very close to our mother. It was Mildred who explained that in our little town Myrle was isolated and considered an outsider. Even if her husband hadn't fallen for another woman, she may well have wanted to flee a place where she was never accepted.

She went first to Oklahoma and then to San Francisco before finally settling in Oregon. Every year or two she'd take a Greyhound to Abbott for a couple of weeks. Those wonderful visits are etched in my mind. I adored my mother. She had a steely strong personality. She had firm opinions. She was also funny and, like Willie, unpredictable. She possessed a get-up-and-go energy that lit up a room. Her confidence was contagious. She made me feel that women could do whatever they wanted. Social restrictions or taboos didn't intimidate her.

People have asked whether I was angry because she left us. The answer is no. Maybe that's because Mama Nelson was all the mother I needed. I did see Myrle Greenhaw as my mom, and I appreciated her. When I later started in with music, she asked me to play for her and praised me to the sky. It would take me many years to realize the positive influence she had on my life. Though I didn't see her often, I felt her presence even in her absence.

I gleaned another insight into my mother when Dad's parents took me to Arkansas to visit their family. Willie was still an infant and too young to come along. That's when I met my maternal grandmother. She was a tiny full-blooded Native American, an exquisite dark-skinned woman with a spiritual aura. She held both my hands and looked deeply into my eyes. The wordless encounter was profound.

Mom's father made whiskey not far from where my father's folks lived. Outlaws were his best customers. My mother would complain about his bootlegging business. She said she hated liquor, but eventually she began drinking herself. I never knew why. In those days, kids didn't ask those sorts of questions.

Mama Nelson's dad—my great-grandfather—was William Smothers, who rode a horse and buggy throughout northern Arkansas as a music instructor. He taught singing. He was frail and bedridden during our visit, but strong enough to point to the bureau so I could admire an old photograph of him as a young man with coal-black hair and a huge handlebar mustache. On the bumpy trip home in a borrowed Model T Ford, Mama Nelson reminisced about her own childhood, during which her brother died real young from alcoholism.

Back in Abbott, we had a pack of Old Maid playing cards, but there was no betting. Drinking and gambling were off-limits. Mama and Daddy Nelson were determined to keep us away from that world. That well may have been the underlying reason they took us under their charge. I have no doubt our father loved us. He had a special love for Willie, as did his second wife, Lorraine. But in watching my grandparents watching my dad, I knew they saw something that frightened them: a dark side. They were committed to saving us from that dark side.

BROTHER

Bobbie, Mama Nelson, and Willie in Abbott

Mama and Daddy Nelson gave Bobbie and me two gifts that saved our lives: love and music. Music and love were one and the same.

Just looking at him, you wouldn't see Daddy Nelson as a music man 'cause he was a blacksmith, big and burly, strong as a bear but gentle as a kitten. He spoke only when he had something to say. Fewer words the better. I'd go out to his shed and watch him sling that heavy anvil like it was light as a feather. Standing with the fire blazing behind him, he pulled out burning-hot metal that he hammered into horse-shoes and precision tools. Farmers all over Hill County came to buy from him.

His skill supported our family. Music supported the family's soul.

It was music in our home and in our church, the Abbott United Methodist. Mama and Daddy Nelson were both students and teachers of music. They were so serious about learning—and making sure we learned—that they ordered books from Chicago showing us the "shape note" method where "do re mi fa so la ti" each had its own symbol. Our earliest musical training was rooted in religion. We were taught music as a form of worship, another way to praise the Lord. Sure, I had a rebellious nature—I've always been a handful—but I never rebelled against God. When Mama and Daddy Nelson told us that just as God had created us, God had also created music, I believed them. Early on, music became my passion. The truth, though, is that I was never a musical prodigy. Not even close.

Bobbie was the prodigy.

SISTER

I see her hands as clearly today as I did eighty years ago. They are the hands of Miss Bertha May, who played the piano at our church. I sat right behind her and watched in wonder. She played all the familiar hymns we loved to sing. I loved watching her fingers fly over the keys. I watched her form the clusters of notes that I'd later learn were chords. I watched her, in short, make magic.

Mama Nelson saw my fascination with the instrument, and so did Miss Bertha. It wasn't long before they let me sit at the piano to see if I could play what I heard. I could. The piano felt like a friend. The instrument responded to my touch. It always had a friendly and inviting feel. It was thrilling when I formed a melody, not through instruction, but by instinct. What was that instinct? Why did I feel such familiarity with this piano? I didn't know then. I don't know now. All I know is that it came effortlessly.

"You're blessed," was all Mama Nelson said.

I was excited by that discovery, but no more excited than Mama and Daddy Nelson. Of all the talents they could have wished for their grandchildren, musical talent was the one that meant the most. When they saw I had natural ability, their encouragement doubled. At first I worried a little that

Willie might be jealous. The truth is that he had nothing to worry about. Willie was born secure. He got as much a kick out of seeing me play piano as anyone. There was never any tension between us. Still isn't.

Even as a little boy, Willie was sharp, but he couldn't be contained. He was so eager to run off that Mama Nelson had to tether him to a pole. I always had to keep an eye on him, chase him down and bring him home. He could be anywhere, hanging with his buddies or wandering to far-off places. Willie was never afraid of getting lost. Willie was never afraid of anything. He was a born explorer. My job was to find him before he got into trouble.

Yet for all his wanderings, he had the patience to sit down and write beautiful poems. That's what set him apart and made us realize there was something different about him. His creative talent was there from the beginning. He was good with rhymes. He could make up metaphors before he even knew the meaning of metaphors. His talent was natural. And his drive to express himself was exceptionally strong. We all were amazed by his way with words.

He was less interested in formal musical training. On the other hand, my grandmother saw that I was willing to learn to read and write music. Our text was the hymnbook. Our at-home instrument was a pump organ. The first song I mastered was "Jesus, Lover of My Soul." That was my gateway to the kingdom of music.

Every Sunday, while Mama Nelson had us in church, where she taught Bible class, Daddy Nelson stayed home. I never asked him why. I was curious, but like I said, we were raised not to question our elders. I never doubted my grandfather's faith, though, especially because of his love of gospel music. The first time I heard live music outside of our church was the day Daddy Nelson took me to Hillsboro, the county seat, to hear a gospel concert.

The Hill County Courthouse looms large in my imagination. It's where I experienced tremendous joy and even greater pain. The joy, in the form of music, came first. The building itself is magnificent. For country folk like us Nelsons, it might as well have been a magic castle. Built at the end of the nineteenth century, the structure is three stories high with a seventy-foot clock tower on top. It's a fancy piece of architecture, highlighted by long columns and an exterior of white limestone that gleams under the burning Texas sun. Inside there's a maze of marble-floor hallways leading to four separate quadrants—courtrooms, a law library, offices for the country officials, and a large auditorium.

I was five when Daddy Nelson first took me to the concert. Willie, then three, was too young. It was exciting to be alone with my grandfather. We didn't have a car and took the inter-urban, a primitive electric railway system that linked little towns across the state. It took only twenty minutes to get to Hillsboro. I'd seen the mighty courthouse before but had never gone inside. When we arrived, the auditorium was already filling up. Daddy Nelson found us seats in the first row. He knew I wanted to be close to the piano player, Miss Martha, who took musical accompaniment to a level I had never heard before.

It was a performance of quartets. Some of the groups— like the Stamps Quartet—were famous. Others were not. But not a single one failed to thrill Daddy Nelson and myself. We knew many of the hymns, of course, but to hear them rendered in precision close harmony added to their allure. I focused on Miss Martha because, unlike Miss May from our

Methodist church, she had a bigger sound and more explosive technique. Our church held a few dozen people. The auditorium held a few hundred. Her piano sounded like a full orchestra. Her chords were more complex, her rhythm more pulsating. During that single concert, she showed me the power of the piano.

I was transformed.

I felt even more transformed when Daddy Nelson did something I never expected. In addition to the quartets singing from the stage, certain people from the audience were selected to lead a sing-along of one of the familiar hymns. That meant, along with Miss Martha, setting the tempo and then waving your hands like a conductor. Before I knew it, my grandfather picked me up and placed me on the stage, where I faced the crowded auditorium. Don't ask me why, but I wasn't scared. I knew the song and didn't hesitate to conduct the audience, who got a kick out of seeing a little girl performing like a grown-up. I especially loved the lyrics that said . . .

You remember songs of heaven
Which you sang with childish voice.
Do you love the hymns they taught you,
Or are songs of earth your choice?

Will the circle be unbroken
By and by, by and by?
There's a better home awaiting
In the sky, in the sky.

Later in life I'd think about that choice, but on that afternoon in Hillsboro I wasn't thinking at all. I was breathing in the voices of what felt like a chorus of angels. I fully expected to float off the stage and fly around the auditorium. It was a heavenly moment.

A few weeks later, Daddy Nelson went to Mr. Kiplinger's general store in Abbott and put $5 down on a $35 old upright German piano that he brought home.

"Play till your heart's content," said my grandfather. And I did.

BROTHER

Bobbie's gift was a source of pride for all of us. She was studious about music. I loved music as much as anyone, but "study" and "Willie" are two words that don't fit together. At the same time, I had an itchin' to play. I'd been writing these little poems and had a funny feeling that the words were supposed to be attached to music.

Then came that sunny day when a package arrived in the mail. Don't wanna sound overly dramatic, but this package changed my life. I opened it up and there it was—a brand-new Stella guitar. Mama and Daddy Nelson, being the beautiful people they were, figured I needed an instrument of my own. So they did what everyone did back then. They got hold of a Sears & Roebuck catalog and found what they were looking for. I wanted a guitar because three of the people I admired most in the world could play: Ernest Tubb, the Texas Troubadour; my father, Ira; and Daddy Nelson himself. Besides, eighty-eight keys were fine for Bobbie but way too many for me. Six strings seemed just 'bout right.

One morning my father came 'round and, seeing that I had this new Stella, started into giving me some instruction.

"I'll teach the boy all he needs to know," my grandfather told his son. He said that, I believe, because he smelled wh key on Dad's breath. Many were the times my father was sent away when his parents suspected he'd been drinking.

No problem, though, for me, 'cause Daddy Nelson turned into a fine teacher. He knew all the basics and patiently showed them to me. I took to the guitar like a duck to water. Not saying I was a virtuoso—still not one—but, without anyone telling me, I knew the guitar had a voice. I knew that box of wood could sing. And I knew by holding it against my chest, it was hearing my heart. It became part of me.

My first heroes were all guitarists. I'd wander down to West, a town six miles south of Abbott, to the Best Movie Theater, where on the big screen were the men I idolized: Roy Rogers, Gene Autry, Tex Ritter, Lash LaRue. Not only were they straight shooters who never failed to bag the bad guys, but they also rode their way through the world singing pretty songs like "Happy Trails to You" and "Back in the Saddle Again" while accompanying themselves on guitar. I also took careful note that their pretty music was usually aimed at pretty girls who looked up at these cowboys with love in their eyes.

Something else in West got my attention and helped widen my world: the Czech community. In Abbott, Mexican families lived across the street from us. We worked the fields together in fellowship and harmony. Never was a racial incident. It was a blessing to be brought up without prejudice. The Czechs who'd settled in West provided still another outlook on life. They spoke with foreign accents, they attended the Catholic church, and, much to my liking, they drank beer. When it came to any kind of booze, the Methodists, Baptists, and Church of Christ constituents of Abbott said no, no, no. Dancing was also frowned upon. So to encounter a people who liked to get buzzed on beer and party with polka bands was great fun.

Mama and Daddy Nelson subscribed to the church teachings and were strict supervisors. At the same time, they knew that Sister and I were natural-born performers. They were keen on us honing those skills. In my case, they saw my feeling for poetry. Rather than read one of my own poems— which were all about puppy love—they arranged for me to recite a spiritual verse at a revival meeting in a nearby town.

Sunny day, picnic food, good folks praising the Lord. Wearing my white sailor suit, hand-sewn by Mama Nelson, I began losing my nerve. Hadn't ever spoken to a big crowd before. Started picking my nose until my nose got all bloody. Blood on my jacket, blood on my little trousers, and me standing at the podium trying to mouth this God-fearing poem. I couldn't. Instead I found myself making up something on the spot that went something like . . . "What are you looking at me for? . . . I got nothing to say. . . . If you don't like the looks of me . . . you can look another way."

From then on, my buddies called me Booger Red. Never was my favorite nickname, but what could I do? I guess it fit.

My outlook on life was pretty rosy. I saw Daddy Nelson as the strongest man in the country. Saw Mama Nelson as the sweetest woman on God's green earth. The earth behind our little house yielded tomatoes, turnips, lettuce, and green peas. We had a couple of hogs and a few calves. Always enough to eat. No money but lots of love.

And of course lots of music. Bobbie's busy learning four new songs a day on the old upright. Mama Nelson's singing her heart out. Daddy Nelson's teaching me how to pluck those six strings. If that isn't enough, we have a little Philco radio that's pulling in stations everywhere from Shreveport to Chicago: Here's Benny Goodman and his big band from the Roseland Ballroom playing "Sing, Sing, Sing." Here's Bob Wills and His Texas Playboys with "San Antonio Rose." The Ink Spots are crooning "If I Didn't Care." Coleman Hawkins is blowing "Body and Soul." I love it all. Swing makes sense, honky-tonk makes sense, jazz makes sense, it all makes me happy, works me up or calms me down—sometimes both at the same time—firing my imagination and soothing my jittery soul.

SISTER

Willie and I played all sorts of games. Let's Pretend was my favorite. We pretended to have a magic carpet. All we had to do was step on this tattered piece of cloth and—*whoosh!*—we were flying up in the sky beyond the clouds to the other side of the moon.

It was a silly game that became an important game, a way for me to protect my little brother from the trauma we experienced in 1939. As an adult, I look back at the year and now realize earth-shattering world events occurred. Germany invaded Poland, marking the start of World War II. America began developing plans for an atomic bomb. Two monumental movies—*Gone with the Wind* and *The Wizard of Oz*—captivated the country. Willie and I saw them both at the Best Movie Theater in West. Yet our awareness was fixated on just one thing: Daddy Nelson became sick.

"What's wrong with him?" I asked Mama.

"Pneumonia," she said.

I didn't understand the word. I didn't want to understand it. I just knew it was something bad. That something went from bad to worse. Daddy Nelson couldn't get out of bed. This was remarkable because nothing had ever stopped this man from doing his work. One day he seemed like the healthiest man on earth, a force of nature. The next day he could hardly move. Within a week's time, I realized what was happening. I was seeing it with my own eyes. Daddy Nelson was dying.

During his last hours, he called me to his bedside. I still hadn't absorbed the reality of his condition. I still assumed he'd get better. But hearing Mama Nelson sob and seeing the concern on the face of Doc Simms, the physician who'd brought me and Willie into the world, shattered my illusion. Daddy Nelson could barely talk. And when he did, he whispered so softly I had to put my ear to his mouth to understand him.

"Play me a song, Bobbie," he said. "Play 'I'll Fly Away.'"

I went to the piano and, as I played, Mama Nelson and Willie found the strength to sing along.

Some glad morning when this life is over
I'll fly away
To a home on God's celestial shore
I'll fly away
When I die, hallelujah, by and by,
When the shadows of this life have gone
I'll fly away
Like a bird from prison bars has flown
Just a few more weary days and then
I'll fly away
To a land where joy shall never end

So great was my grief that I blocked out the details of his funeral and burial. All I can remember is Mama Nelson keeping us close to her and me keeping Willie close to me. Our grandfather loved me with all his heart, but his relationship to his grandson was on another level. They were incredibly close. Alfred Nelson was the most important man in Willie's life. Our father, Ira, for all his good qualities, was no one we could count on. Daddy Nelson was the opposite. He supported us emotionally and financially; we couldn't imagine the world without him.

His sudden death at age fifty-six reverberated in two separate ways, one worse than the other. We had to face death itself. Willie was six, I was eight, and we presumed everyone would live forever—especially Daddy Nelson, who seemed indestructible. The second shock, the one that frightened us most, was the real possibility of losing Mama Nelson, even though she remained alive. Authorities made it clear to our grandmother that we might have to go into a foster home or, even scarier, be forced into separate homes.

The reason was made clear: Mama Nelson didn't have the means to support us. Our father and mother were living their own lives and in no position to reclaim us. The county was legally obligated to protect us. They knew we were not supported by our biological parents. As long as Daddy Nelson was alive, the authorities didn't think twice about our welfare because they knew that he made a living. Now that our grandfather was gone, they questioned our grandmother's ability to house and feed us. Daddy Nelson's blacksmith work was our only source of income. With two young children completely dependent on her, how could Mama Nelson possibly get by?

For weeks, I was a basket case. The minute I saw the authorities, I grabbed Willie and said, "We gotta hide."

"Why?" he wanted to know.

"You don't have to know. You just have to listen to me."

We hid in a ditch behind our house while men in suits questioned Mama Nelson. We stayed out of sight until the authorities left. A couple of times when I heard voices raised and thought people were actually coming to get us, Willie and I scampered into the fields and hid in the corn and cotton. They weren't going to take us away from Mama Nelson. They weren't going to separate me from my brother. I'd never let that happen.

BROTHER

Daddy Nelson's death hit me hard. I had this feeling that he had been stolen from us. We had been cheated. It felt cruel and unfair. But if I didn't fall apart, it was because of Sister. She let me know that nothing was going to happen to me. She made it clear that we'd get through this thing together. I don't know where she got that confidence and strength. All I do know is that I needed reassurance in the worst way. And Bobbie had it.

"Mama Nelson's never gonna let anything happen to us," Bobbie kept saying.

I have blurry memories of our hiding out when it seemed like the law might snatch us up. I didn't understand what was going on, but I trusted Bobbie. She kept saying it was a game we were going to win. She had faith. She gave me faith.

She promised me that our life wouldn't be ruined.

SISTER

Bobbie as Sophomore Princess, age fourteen, 1945

Our life was based on faith. After Daddy Nelson died, we had nothing else to go on. During this period of uncertainty, I tried real hard to keep fear away from Willie. I kept reassuring him. Those times when we hid in the ditch or ran off into the fields, and I treated it like an adventure, on the outside I was composed, but on the inside I was a mess.

Then one day I overheard Mama Nelson speaking to the county authorities. They came to the house to interview her. I was outside, but with the back door open, I could hear every word. There were two men. Both spoke impatiently, even belligerently. I got the idea that they were there to declare her unfit to remain our legal guardian. They asked questions about why our mother had left us; why our father left us; and how could she, without a job, possibly support us.

Mama Nelson's answers were straight to the point. She had only good things to say about her son and daughter-in-law. They simply lacked the maturity to raise children. She and her late husband had embodied that maturity. Even though he was gone, she had not the slightest doubt that she could manage. Finances didn't concern her because, she explained, the eggs from our chickens could be used to barter necessities from Mr. Kiplinger's general store. Beyond that, she could give music lessons to children in the area. Most important, she was of strong mind and body and would work the fields herself. She had picked cotton and corn before and would do it again. She would guard her grandchildren against all harm, see to their ongoing education in the Abbott public school, and make absolutely certain that they attended the Methodist church every Wednesday for Bible class and every Sunday for services.

Mama Nelson summarized her case with a single sentence: "My grandchildren will never miss a meal or suffer from neglect."

The men's attitude changed. Where at first their tone had been harsh, they now spoke respectfully. They had no questions and I had no more fear. My grandmother won the day. We were safe.

Mama Nelson never dated or remarried. She was a one-man woman, and once that man was gone, we became her sole focus. Early on, she enlisted our help in tending to the garden where we grew our own vegetables. She made good on her promise and successfully traded our chickens' eggs for staples from Mr. Kiplinger. She found a few students to whom she taught piano and singing. And, without hesitation, she went to work in the fields. Appreciating her dedication to us, Willie and I were eager to help. None of us minded manual labor.

In the evening, we came home from picking cotton. We were tired but satisfied for having done a good day's work. We were taught to be grateful.

"God gave us the strength to work these fields," said our grandmother, "and we give him praise for that strength." Preparing our dinner, Mama Nelson sang hymns of praise. Her voice filled the house with love. After we ate, she sat in her rocking chair as she read the Bible, her long lustrous hair spilling over the back of the chair. She taught me to braid her hair and I, in turn, taught Willie. We took turns braiding our grandmother's hair.

It became a ritual.

BROTHER

I liked farming. With Daddy Nelson gone, farming became a big part of our life. We farmed to survive. I dug in. I joined the Future Farmers of America, a group that was strong in rural communities during and after the Depression. I got a kick out of planting and picking the lettuce, carrots, turnips, and green beans. Working the fields became something of a competition. I wanted to wind up with the biggest bag of cotton.

I related to the animals. Still do. I had a heart for hogs. Loved watching them in the muddy pen. Each one had a different personality. They're smart animals. Discovered that they're as trainable as dogs. You can teach them to sit, stand, shake your hand, and do all sorts of tricks. People don't realize that.

Love horses, too. Didn't have one, but I'd get lucky and borrow a neighbor's horse for an hour or two. Riding came naturally. Sitting atop that streamlined, strong animal made me feel streamlined and strong by extension. Me and the horse were one. Might sound crazy, but there was a soul-to-soul connection. Of course in the movies I'd seen Roy Rogers's Trigger and Hopalong Cassidy's Topper. You couldn't separate these horses from the heroes who rode them. Horses are sacred.

Sacred songs—the hymns I learned at church and from Mama Nelson—were songs I always loved. I was christened by the Abbott United Methodist Women's Missionary Society as a baby. Later I learned that was because they thought I'd become a missionary. Don't know what gave them that idea.

As a kid, if I had any mission at all, it was about being mischievous. I like stirring up a little trouble. I was out there poking bumblebee nests with a stick just for the hell of it. Reading Charles Atlas ads in comic books, I sent off for his pamphlets about getting strong. When I got into scraps, I managed to get in my blows. I liked a good fight. I liked team sports as well and was a proud member of the Abbott Fighting Panthers, playing baseball and basketball and running track. Did a stint as quarterback on our football team. That was tricky 'cause our field was filled with rocks. That went a long way to toughening me up.

I thought smoking gave me a tough look. Loving to smoke and loving the Lord didn't go together in the eyes of many churchgoers. Personally, I thought they went together just fine. Never saw the contradiction in being mischievous and being a believer. If you can believe it, I started out smoking strips of cedar bark. Tobacco came later. And after that a certain substance I credit with saving my life. But I don't wanna get ahead of the story.

Puppy love came early. Music helped. In fostering romance, music always helps. Before we were teenagers, Bobbie and I were good enough to play at the school dances. That got me female attention. And female attention was something I always enjoyed.

SISTER

It took me a while to play music outside church. I gained a reputation in Hill County and was asked to perform in tent meetings, many held out in the country. For a long time, even though our economic situation was dire, I wouldn't accept money. Didn't seem right. I loved the spirit of those revivals. If my piano contributed to that spirit, that was payment enough. Since God's love is free, I felt that God's music should be free as well.

It's amazing that given the different denominations in Abbott—Methodist, Baptist, Catholic, Church of God in Christ—everyone got along. I don't want to idealize, though, because I did encounter prejudice. When Willie and I started working the fields alongside Mexican and African American folks, we became friends with those kids. It seemed only natural for me to invite them to hear me play piano in church. But I soon learned that they weren't exactly welcome where I worshipped. That confused me. I wanted to have my good friends see me play. I was proud of my playing. But more than that, I wanted to feel that my church had compassion and love for everyone. Why were they excluded from the place where I worshipped? I never stopped attending Abbott United Methodist, but the incident did get me to thinking about challenging conventional church dogma.

At the same time, I was hardly a rebellious girl. Like Willie, I loved sports, especially basketball, and played on the school teams. I don't want to brag, but my brother and I were among the most well-liked kids. We got along with everyone, and our musical talents added to our popularity.

School also provided the big break in our finances. The egg-bartering, vegetable-growing, cotton-picking, hay-baling way of living was nerve-racking. Mama Nelson had a few music students, but I don't think their parents paid more than a quarter for an hour's lesson. We were always up against it. Often our meals were minimal. The big change came when we heard our public school needed someone to work in the cafeteria. Mama Nelson grabbed that job, knowing that, given all the leftovers from the lunchtime meal, we'd never go hungry. And we never did.

Mama Nelson protected us from the fear of starvation. But when I was a young girl listening to the radio, the reality of World War II struck another kind of fear in my heart. On December 7, 1941, the Japanese bombed Pearl Harbor. That terrified me. Mama Nelson could see that, and she would quote President Roosevelt's earlier statement that all we have to fear is fear itself. But that didn't help because I was afraid of fear, too. My fears didn't disappear. Truth is, I was anxious all during the war years of the forties. Every time I heard a plane fly overhead, I was scared it was a Japanese or German bomber about to blow us up.

BROTHER

The war was like something out of a storybook, only it was a real-life event. It was exciting to follow the news on the radio. In my naïve way, it felt like listening to *Dick Tracy* or *Terry and the Pirates.* I had no doubt that the good guys—the Allies—would win. Part of me wished I were older so I could go off and fight. Several Abbott boys went to war and returned not only as grown men but as heroes.

The forties were a heroic decade with a clear line between good and evil. The American story seemed simple still. With the advent of the Cold War and generational divides, the fifties and sixties would complicate that story. But as a product of the forties, I saw the world in basic terms. We were on the right side of history. Much later I'd have grave doubts about my country's methods and motives, but as a kid I was a patriot. *Jack Armstrong, the All-American Boy* was my show. It was a radio program all about catching villains. The hero always got his man. Jack Armstrong was my hero.

I freely associated Hoot Gibson, Wild Bill Elliott, and Tom Mix with General Patton, General Eisenhower, and Winston Churchill. The battles were on, and the bad guys didn't have a prayer.

Don't know where all that optimism came from. Do know, though, that the small world of Abbott strengthened my resolve in a couple of ways. First, just because Abbott was so small, I was hungry to see beyond the bend. And second, because Abbott folks had such a high regard for Sister and me, I got to feeling that I could handle myself no matter what I might find beyond the bend. I believe that high regard was due to our skill at music and sports. It didn't hurt that we had friendly personalities. Sometimes just being nice can go a long way.

I always felt like I had the support of the small rural community I called home. That support gave me the confidence to face the tough times ahead.

SISTER

Bobbie and Willie, 1946

Just outside Abbott was a structure called the Tabernacle. It was an open-air sanctuary with a makeshift roof held up by poles. That's where members of different churches showed up for revival meetings. I played there on a regular basis.

By the time I became a teenager, my technique as a pianist had improved. That's because Mama Nelson had turned my instruction over to Margaret Gardner, an accomplished musician who saw my potential. She ordered instruction books that came all the way from Theodore Presser music publishers in Bryn Mawr, Pennsylvania. I took those books to heart and worked my way through every one of them, determined to learn as many compositions and styles as possible. Miss Gardner was the kind of teacher who didn't believe in scolding. She was an encourager.

At some point, I did start earning a little money. The ministers involved knew I was being raised by my widowed grandmother and offered me a few dollars from the collection plate. When I hesitated, they insisted. I put together $15 and decided to buy a typewriter since I'd be taking typing my sophomore year. I had my eye on a brand-new 1944 Underwood. Alone, I took the interurban train to Waco, a midsize city that, to me, might as well have been New York. I was a country girl who didn't know the first thing about urban environments. I didn't know there were good and bad parts of a city. That's how I wound up in the wrong part of town. A policeman, seeing this innocent teenage girl, asked me if I was lost. I admitted that I was. He kindly escorted me to the business district, where I found what I was looking for. At times I was certain angels were protecting me; at other times, I've felt completely unprotected. I guess that's just how it goes for us all.

Typing became another skill I savored. I related it to piano playing. It was another keyboard that required dexterity. It wasn't long before I was clicking away. I loved engaging the lever and moving the carriage along the length of the machine so I could hear that ever-satisfying ting of the bell. Little did I know that typing, like piano playing, would turn out to be instrumental to my survival.

Two events in my childhood—my parents' departure and Daddy Nelson's death—had threatened my emotional survival. I was frightened that I simply couldn't go on. But with age, the fear diminished largely because of Mama Nelson's protective presence. But it's also because my church life, along with school life, was so satisfying. Both those lives were bolstered by music. Sunday services and school proms made me feel good about myself. For all her spiritual devotion, Mama Nelson never forbade me and Willie from playing dance music. She and Daddy Nelson were the first to show us how to harmonize—he on guitar and me on piano—so it was an easy transition from "What a Friend We Have in Jesus" to "Waltz Across Texas." I liked all the styles, and Willie had proven to be a good singer. So if our peers wanted to boogie-woogie or jitterbug, my brother and I could get 'em going.

In the dating department, Willie was far ahead of me. I liked a lot of the boys at our school, and I believe some liked me, but I never did go out with any of them. I suppose I was too reserved. I wasn't ready for romance.

Willie was born ready.

BROTHER

I got along great with members of the opposite sex until I started marrying them."

For years that was my standard line. There's great truth to it, especially in my early life.

The deeper truth, though, is that love, sex, and romance were all interconnected. I loved love, I loved sex, I loved romance. The three usually overlapped. Getting halfway decent at the guitar and finding the nerve to croon in front of a crowd added fuel to the fire. I'm not saying that I started playing to attract girls, but when I saw how my playing could also be a form of flirtation, I flirted like crazy. Even without music I would have been a lovestruck fool. But music—with its sensual power—made me twice as foolish. When it came to winning over women, I didn't hesitate to use the built-in advantage of being a performer.

Another advantage: Playing music onstage meant I didn't have to risk rejection. I didn't have to ask anyone to dance. I didn't have to take a chance in approaching a girl who might not want to be approached. Lots of times girls approached me. That made things easier.

Still remember my first case of puppy love. Ramona Stafford. Sweet as she could be. On a sunny September day, she and I jumped on the interurban and rode all the way up to

Dallas so I could take her to the Texas State Fair. When she agreed to go into the Tunnel of Love, I sat next to her in that little car and made my move. I put my arm around her. I was hoping—hell, I was praying—she'd turn her mouth toward mine. She didn't. My first real kiss was a ways off. But I was already in love with love, and for the rest of my life, I'd be chasing romance—or was romance chasing me?

PART II

THE STORY CHANGES...

SISTER

Arlyn Bud Fletcher changed my life and Willie's as well. The day I met Bud Fletcher proved to be monumental.

It happened in 1947. Brother Wayne Dunson had recruited me to play for his revivals. He was an ambitious preacher looking to spread the gospel all over the state. One Sunday he held services at the Methodist church in Vaughan, a small community on the outskirts of Hillsboro. One of the deacons, Fred Fletcher, who had recently been elected county road commissioner, was in attendance. He brought along his son, Bud, who had fought in World War II on the Italian front. His face bore a pronounced scar. I thought it was from the war, but I later learned it was there from birth. The scar didn't bother me. When Brother Dunson introduced me to Deacon Fletcher, his wife, three daughters, and son, I felt an immediate attraction to Bud. A tall man of impressive stature, Bud radiated strength. His hair was dark, his eyes bright, his personality jovial.

"I'm looking at the prettiest girl in all of Texas," he said.

I blushed.

Then he said blushing made me look even prettier. My blush deepened. Bud's smile widened. His flattery didn't feel false. I took it to heart. No man had ever made me feel that way before or since. Right there in church, he asked me out on a date. Truth was, I'd never been on a date. I was flabbergasted. He was polite and charming and wouldn't take no for an answer. For all my reservations, I still said yes.

We met in April and married in August.

More than seventy years later, I'm still a little shocked when I remember that our courtship lasted no longer than five months. Bud was twenty-two, I was sixteen, the same age as when my parents married. He was a grown man. I was a girl.

I was hopelessly naïve. I say that because I had no sex education from either my mother, grandmother, or school. My cousin Mildred had helped me through menstruation, but when I met Bud, she was already out of the house, married, and had a child of her own. When it came to men, and especially mature men, I didn't have a clue.

He took me to a honky-tonk called Shadowland. My first date and also my first honky-tonk. I was more than a little overwhelmed. Bud slipped a nickel in the jukebox and played "Sentimental Journey." I didn't know how to dance, but, boy, he sure did. I didn't know the first thing about sweet talk. But, yes, Bud was a sweet talker. I saw him as a sweet man. He didn't pressure me, didn't rush me or try to go too far. I saw he was a drinker, but so was my dad. In fact, my father knew Bud and liked him just fine. That made Bud more acceptable to me. Only later would I learn how liquor could destroy a life. Back then it was simply something that people did. Our preacher preached against it; our grandparents didn't like it one bit; but the rest of the world treated it as normal.

Bud's way with me was always respectful. No man had ever showered me with such attention and affection. Naturally I was flattered. But I was also new at this. And alone. No matter how close I was with Willie, my feelings about Bud—or his for me—weren't something I'd discuss with my brother. All throughout our lives, we kept our distance from each other's romantic entanglements. Maybe that's why we've gotten along so well.

Even though I was a novice when it came to men, Bud and I got along beautifully. There were no disagreements, no tension, and surprisingly no reservations on my part. Looking back, I see it now as I saw it then: It was love, pure and simple. Well, maybe "simple" is the wrong word. "Love" is certainly the right word. And so is "pure." For all the drama that would ensue, I know my attraction to Bud was based on what I saw as the beauty of his soul. Deep down he was a good man. He was the great love of my life. He had an abundance of positive energy. I have not the slightest doubt that he loved me completely. I was naïve enough to think that such a love would lead to a lifetime of happiness. I was naïve about everything.

And yet . . .

I see him as he was back then. A man brimming with charm. A man who loved music and would listen to music night and day. A man who loved not only me, but Willie as well. He saw our talent and wanted the world to see it. He was the first one to enter our lives with a vision. He was part of that vision. Though he wasn't a musician, he had the confidence to lead a band. And he did. That was the band that kicked off the brother/sister professional relationship.

Willie and I lived in a sheltered world of childhood. Bud lived in the wide-open world of adulthood. He ushered us into his world, and both of us were more than willing to go there. We were thrilled.

BROTHER

First time I got paid to make music was with John Rejcek's fifteen-member family polka band. Couldn't have been older than eleven. Strumming my Stella guitar, I was surrounded by fiddles, tubas, trumpets, and drummers. I had a blast. Not sure how much I contributed to the overall sound, but Mr. Rejcek liked me and let me play along. The gigs were mainly at dance halls in West and Waco where the Czech community turned out in force. I wasn't even a teen-ager, but because I was standing way in the back of the band, club owners didn't seem to care.

I loved looking out at the crowd and seeing everyone dancing up a storm. At this tender age, I already knew this was what I wanted to do. Everything about music felt right. Even music from a foreign land sung in a foreign language didn't feel foreign to me. I got into it. Made me feel good, not only to play it, but to watch folks dancing their polkas and waltzing their worries away. What could be better?

Well, I knew Mama Nelson didn't feel that way. She didn't approve of dancing, drinking, and smoking.

I never lied to my grandmother. So shortly after joining John Rejcek, I told her the truth. I was part of a band.

"What kind of music are you playing?"

"Mainly polkas."

She waited a long time before asking the next question.

"And there's dancing going on?"

"Yes, ma'am."

"And drinking?"

"Yes, ma'am."

"But you aren't doing any of the drinking, are you?"

"No, ma'am."

"And you're too busy playing your guitar to be dancing."

"Yes, ma'am."

"I still don't like it."

"I didn't think you would."

"And I wish you wouldn't do it."

"But there is something good about it."

"What's that?" she asked.

I handed her eight dollars.

"How long did you have to work to get this money?"

"One night."

I didn't have to remind her that eight dollars was my pay for working the fields for a week. I could see that Mama Nelson was shocked. She shook her head from side to side, sighed a deep sigh, and then accepted the money. I never did get her approval, but I also didn't get any flak.

When Bud Fletcher came along, I was hardly a seasoned veteran. I was a scrappy thirteen-year-old kid in love with every kind of music coming out of our little Philco. Bing Crosby. Louis Armstrong. Floyd Tillman. Roy Acuff. Jack Teagarden. And especially Bob Wills and His Texas Playboys.

Bud and I bonded over Bob Wills. Bob was Bud's idol. Mine too. And I think Bud saw himself as Bob. The difference, of course, was that Bob was a genuine musician and songwriter. He played fiddle, wrote songs, and was called the King of Western Swing for good reason. He invented the genre that wed country to jazz rhythms. Like me, he loved African American music and was influenced by its feel. His singer, Tommy Duncan, had a natural conversational style that had a big impact on me.

You don't have to be a musician to love music with the passion of a musician. Essentially a nonmusician, Bud had that passion. But he had more. He had charisma. He liked attention. He liked the idea of standing in front of a band and waving his arms like he was leading it.

He was a showman, but mostly he was a hustler.

He saw that I had hustle energy as well. He had the drive to get things done. He had follow-through. He made it happen. Later in life, I'd meet other guys good at promotion. I'd also develop my own style of self-promotion. But Bud was the first to show me how to break through the status quo and turn a dream into reality. His dream was to have a band of his own. His other dream was to marry my sister. That's saying something since, six years younger than him, she was the most popular girl at our school. When they met, she was still only a junior. She was also a church girl who continued to be watched over by Mama Nelson.

Bud knew all this. But he wanted Bobbie, and he wanted this band, and Bud was someone who got what he wanted.

SISTER

On Mama and Daddy Nelson's porch: Bobbie and Bud Fletcher (standing),
cousin Ronnie, Willie (holding dog), cousin Ernestine

Bud wanted to have sex right away. I understood. I was experiencing a strong sexual awakening, but my upbringing was stronger than my desire. Sex before marriage would bring too much guilt. When I told him that, he understood and gently backed off. My refusal, I believe, may have also sped up his proposal. Seems kind of obvious now.

"I want to sit across the table from you every morning," he said. "I want to marry you."

At first I didn't say yes. I was conflicted. I did want to marry him. I did want to make love. But I also had a world of interests. Next year I'd be a senior. I loved school. I loved being on the basketball team. I loved playing hymns in church. I loved playing revivals for Brother Dunson. I had so much going on in my young life that the consideration of marriage—at least before meeting Bud—was the last thing on my mind.

"There's nothing you have to give up," he insisted. "I want you to keep playing in church. I also want you to enjoy your senior year. There's no reason you can't graduate."

"There's never been a married woman who's gone to Abbott High," I said.

"You'll make history. You'll be the first."

"I'll feel strange. I'm not ready for marriage."

"But marriage," Bud argued, "is ready for you."

"How can you be so sure?"

"I see it in your eyes, Bobbie. And you can feel it in your heart, can't you?"

I could but wasn't willing to admit it. But Bud was persuasive. He wasn't about to give up. He also had a strong ally—my dad. I don't actually know why, but my father wanted to marry me off. Those were the days when fathers were still looking to marry off their daughters to families with money. For Dad, Bud was perfect for me. He made it clear that he favored the union. Later Dad also was eager to do the bidding of Bud's parents, Mr. and Mrs. Fletcher. They were influential in the community, and Dad thought my connection to them would help all of us prosper.

Willie liked the idea of Bud as his brother-in-law. Bud was already acting like Willie's big brother. When, for example,

Bud picked me up for a date to watch him play softball, he'd bring Willie along. Willie joined the team. In Willie's eyes, Bud could do no wrong. And Bud felt the same about Willie.

Mama Nelson had her objections. She thought I was too young. And she also didn't like the fact that Bud drank. She saw, though, that I had fallen in love. She knew that history has a way of repeating itself. As I said, my mother and father were sixteen when they married. Now it was my turn. It started to feel inevitable. Always a practical woman, Mama Nelson understood that she couldn't control young people. She was too smart to forbid me to marry and endanger my warm and loving feelings for her. She protected our relationship by not getting in the way. It didn't take long for my reservations to melt away. Sure, I'd be the only married girl in high school, but I could deal with that. I had met the man who would make me happy for the rest of my life. I couldn't deny that I wanted to be with him night and day.

So less than five short months after that first fateful meeting, Bud and I married in a Methodist church in Waco. The day remains something of a blur. I don't know why, but Mama Nelson and Willie weren't there. I can't say why the ceremony wasn't held in my home church in Abbott. All I do remember is that Commissioner Fletcher and his wife were in attendance. So were my father and his second wife, Lorraine.

Bud and I consummated our love that night. That was beautiful. I was grateful to have waited. There was nothing to be guilty about. We moved in with Bud's parents at their home in Vaughan. Bud honored his word and encouraged me to complete my senior year. A school bus came to fetch me every morning. I kept up with my studies, my piano playing, and my typing. I gave up basketball only because I was afraid of hurting my hands. Even then I saw my hands as the key to my future. My friends might have found it strange that I'd become a married woman, but they treated me no differently than before. My grades were good. And come May, I did graduate. During my senior year, though, something else happened that shaped the future of my brother and myself. Bud started a band.

BROTHER

He called it Bud Fletcher and the Texans. The main Texans—at least the ones playing most of the music—were me and Sister. To be honest, I gotta put Sister first. Bobbie was by far the most accomplished musician. Not only could she read and write music flawlessly, she could work in any style. She'd hear a song once on the radio and be able to play it back. She could also teach it to us and work out an arrangement for the band, no easy task 'cause none of us were literate in music. My dad, a good fiddler who could double on guitar, joined us on the bandstand most weekends. I was happy to have him along for the ride. Bud, too. Bud was crazy about his father-in-law. Our biology teacher, Glen Ellison, played trombone well enough to fill out our sound. That was great until the principal of Abbott High learned that one of its instructors was in a bar band. Poor Glen lost his teaching job.

Bud tried playing bass fiddle and never quite got the hang of it, but he did learn to drum and got pretty good. His musical ability didn't really matter because Bud had what it took to be the front man. He was great at entertaining the crowd with funny remarks. He could wave his hands like Cab Calloway and get folks to dancing. He was a ringleader whose main talent was getting us gigs. He booked us into joints like the Avalon Club and Scenic Wonderland in Waco. He also found us work closer to home in West and Hillsboro.

I was with Bud when he marched into radio station WACO and demanded to speak to the manager.

"I hear y'all run a talent contest," he said.

"We sure do," the manager confirmed.

"Well, I got me two of the most talented young musicians in all of Texas. Put 'em on the air and I guarantee you your listeners are gonna love 'em. Got a hundred bucks that says they'll win any contest hands down."

"I'm no gambler," said the manager, "but if they're as good as you say they are, I'll give 'em a shot."

Week later, we were on the air. Our competitors were yo-delers and banjo players and fiddlers. Back then, there was a whole lot of talent in rural Texas towns. Yet Bobbie and I carried the day. We won the damn contest.

That emboldened Bud to go to KHBR, the station operating out of Hillsboro, and convince them that Bud Fletcher and the Texans needed a quarter-hour show of our own. Suddenly, in our small fishpond, we were halfway famous. Some gals at school even started a Willie Nelson fan club.

SISTER

Willie and his women is a subject that requires a book of its own. I'm not here to write that book, but only to say that the girls loved my brother. I guess it's his God-given easygoing charm, or the sparkle in his eye, or how, when you talk to him, he makes you feel like the most important person in the world. I think he likes flirting. I know he does. But he didn't even need to flirt. Back in those days when females weren't supposed to be aggressive, girls were so fast to flirt with Willie they'd wind up fighting over him. He liked that. What man wouldn't?

I can't tell you how many girls approached me for advice about the best way to approach Willie. I never gave out any advice. When it came to women, Willie had his own way. He had lots of choices, and the last thing in the world he needed was me meddling in his business. So I never did.

BROTHER

When you grow up in a little rural town, you aren't exposed to much. Your world is small. And if you meet someone who grew up in that same world but somehow developed a bigger vision, that makes a huge impression. Bud's hometown, Vaughan, was really no different than my hometown of Abbott. Yet Bud had ventured out, joined the army, and come home with all these big-time ideas. He became my first real role model of what it means to fearlessly promote yourself. He worked his game without apology. He told folks we were so good that everyone in Texas needed to know about us. He won over tough guys who ran beer parlors and sawdust-on-the-floor roadhouses. He talked radio station owners into putting us on the air.

After a gig, Bud would say, "Willie, you're going places."

"Like where?"

"Like wherever you want. It's a big world out there and you need to see it. You need to taste it. You need to think big."

At the time, of course, I was thinking small. Wasn't thinking any further than getting paid for a Friday night's worth of work. But Bud was thinking ahead. He had his moves. I studied those moves. I saw that if I was gonna make my way in music, he was paving the path I'd have to follow. He was showing me how to be bold. Don't worry who ignores or rejects you. Just keep at it. Keep going. Wear 'em down.

And shoot for the stars. One night, for instance, me and Bud were talking about how great it'd be to bring Bob Wills and His Texas Playboys to Hill County to play in our backyard. Bob Wills was to country music what Louis Armstrong was to jazz. The great innovator. I idolized him.

"How in hell we ever gonna get Bob Wills to play Hill County?" I asked Bud.

"Guarantee Bob a fee. Find a venue. Sell tickets. Become a promoter."

"I'm no promoter."

"Maybe you weren't yesterday, but you are today. I'm officially promoting you from guitar picker to promoter."

I accepted the promotion. Bud had enough guts for both of us. Besides, just the idea of seeing Bob Wills live and in person was enough to get me going. A legend like Jimmie Rodgers, whose music I loved, was already gone. Wills was a living legend.

Bud and I pulled it off, although we didn't make a cent. We rented an outdoor pavilion at Lake Whitney, twenty miles from Abbott. Beautiful spot. We agreed on Wills's fee, a thousand dollars—in those days a fortune. What in the world gave me the nerve to think we'd be able to cover that cost? Bud Fletcher. When it came to taking chances, Bud never questioned a thing. The idea of asking Wills to reduce his price was out of the question. As an artist, I put him up there with Bix Beiderbecke. As a writer, he was in the same league as Hoagy Carmichael. Wills had composed songs that other great bandleaders like Adolph Hofner and Dewey Groom had covered. He was also an innovator. Months after he hired

Johnny Gimble on electric mandolin, country bands everywhere started using mandolins.

Bud and I spent weeks planning the big event. We plastered posters over every last hamlet in Hill County. I publicized the show on our Hillsboro radio station, where Bobbie and I played our own versions of Bob Wills hits like "Stay All Night" and "Sugar Moon." The night of the show, the full moon was shining on the shimmering Texas lake. Wills and his boys played their hearts out. I loved every minute of their show. Fans showed in the hundreds, but Bud and I barely covered expenses. No profit, but lots of gain. The main gain was the lesson I learned about stage presentation. Wills kept singing for hours on end—"Trouble in Mind," "Stay All Night," "Bubbles in My Beer"—with no breaks, no bs between songs, no silly banter, just music music music. His show had a flow. He had this sixth sense about how to keep the show going from weepy ballads to yodeling waltzes to honky-tonk stompers. No one left unsatisfied. Every single minute he was onstage, Bob Wills was all about the business of engaging his fans. That's the business I wanted to be in.

SISTER

At first it was beautiful. Bud had brought together me, Willie, and our dad in a band. Only Bud could have done that. He understood that, no matter how painful my early years might have been, no matter how I was traumatized by my parents leaving or Daddy Nelson dying, music was my greatest comfort. Music was what held our family together. And I loved how Bud loved Willie. He saw my brother's genius and did all he could to bring it out.

I remember Bud and I marveling at how, as a young kid, Brother had put together his own songbook. On the cover, he even drew the "n" in "Songs" to look like a horse. He'd written twelve songs with titles like "Faded Love and Wasted Dream" and "I Guess I Was Born to Be Blue." He was wiser than his years and, from the start, understood how romantic despair helped sell a song. That would always be one of Willie's trademarks.

Mama Nelson watched all this from afar. She never once came into a barroom to see Bud Fletcher and the Texans. We didn't expect her to. Actually, Willie and I expected her to give us a hard time about playing for drinkers. But she didn't. She didn't have to. We knew how she felt, and she was wise enough to leave well enough alone. She was not a controlling woman. She understood that God works in mysterious ways and, though her faith was iron strong, she never tried to take over our lives.

I knew my minister and other church folk disapproved of my prominent position in the band. It was actually double disapproval. First, they thought I was playing the devil's music and had no business in barrooms; and second, they considered it risqué for a woman to be in an otherwise all-male group. The second objection seemed silly, since the group's leader was my husband. I didn't hear anyone complaining about Dale Evans performing with Roy Rogers. I also didn't believe that popular music was satanic. I shared my brother's love of popular music. I'd grown up on composers like George Gershwin and Cole Porter, whose work was beautiful. I'd always been enchanted by the lush melodies and poetic lyrics to songs like "My Funny Valentine," "Night and Day," "Body and Soul," and "Fools Rush In." I didn't hear devils in that music. I heard angels. I also heard a godly spirit in country music. Hank Williams, for instance, sang from the heart. His songs had a prayerful quality. The fact that he addressed worldly concerns didn't make him any less spiritual.

Even as a teenager, I had a wide and respectful view of the majesty of all music. From my piano bench, I looked out at the crowd and got happy when our dance numbers got them moving. These were hardworking people looking to escape the tedium of their daily lives. I was pleased to be part of a band that brought them pleasure and even joy, and my ability to switch styles at the drop of a hat did wonders for my self-esteem. My fellow bandmates were quick to compliment me. I loved the spontaneity of playing with others. Because we all knew and loved jazz, we also were able to improvise our way through all sorts of songs. The process of making-it-up-as-you-go-along was always thrilling.

Just as I had made good on my promise to graduate from high school, Willie kept his pledge to Mama Nelson and, two years after me, graduated as well. He still played sports. And he was still the most popular guy in school.

Bud's band never got in the way. In fact, we expanded. We found a great drummer, Whistle Watson, who was also a showman, and a great singer, Ed Knapp. Willie also did some singing, but Ed, being a grown-up, had more experience in pleasing an audience. And our dad was still on fiddle. The money wasn't great—those barrooms and dance halls didn't pay much—but we earned a strong reputation. At a very young age, Willie and I became professional musicians.

BROTHER

*Bud Fletcher and the Texans: Willie (with guitar on far left);
Bobbie (seated); Ira Nelson, Bobbie and Willie's dad (with
fiddle); Bud Fletcher (next to Ira)*

Given how easy it is for local bands to fall apart, Bud
Fletcher and the Texans had a long run—a good five
years thanks to Bud's charisma as our leader and Bobbie's role
as our piano player. Not every country band back then had a
piano player. We were blessed because Bobbie grounded our
sound. She was our foundation. All the instruments have
their place. I've been holding a guitar next to my heart since I
got that first Stella. I love it like a father loves his child. But

piano is the mother of all instruments. On the piano, you can create clusters of complex chords; you can create all sorts of rhythm patterns; and you can approximate the feel of a whole orchestra. If your piano player really has solid technique and the ability to switch styles, you're lucky. We were definitely lucky to have Bobbie. Sister never looked to be in the spotlight, but she was our secret weapon.

SISTER

I saw the danger but ignored it. Mama Nelson saw it as well and warned me about it in no uncertain terms. It was Bud's drinking. Mama Nelson knew that her son's drinking had damaged my parents' marriage. And she observed that, hanging out with Bud and our dad, Willie had started drinking. She hated any kind of booze—beer, liquor, or wine made no difference to her. I understood her attitude. But I also didn't want to admit how drinking was adversely affecting my marriage.

I wanted to pretend it wasn't a problem.

My dad's drinking didn't bother me 'cause he wasn't a crazy drunk. Far as Brother goes, Willie, like most teenage boys, was looking for a little buzz now and then. I didn't see any harm in that. Besides, Willie could do no wrong.

But Bud was different. His drinking turned him into another person. He got short-tempered. He could be violent. Bud was in one barroom brawl after another. I never knew the reasons he fought. I'm not sure there were any. He just got punch-drunk. Things got worse for me when he wouldn't come home when he said he would. On a weekday night, I'd wait up for him till ten, eleven, midnight, and beyond, only to fall asleep alone. He'd turn up the next morning, or maybe the morning after. Then he began disappearing for days on end.

I was still a teenager and not the kind of young woman who could confront a man. It was a different time, a different era. I loved Bud and, despite everything, I saw the goodness of his heart. Even if I had found the courage to leave him because of his rowdiness, something would have stopped me, something that changed the very nature of our marriage. I was pregnant.

It was welcome news. Bud was happy to be a dad; Willie was happy to be an uncle; my dad was happy to be a granddad; and Mama Nelson was happy to be a great-grandma. When my mother heard about it, she called and gave me her support. I hardly felt alone.

Pregnancy, though, didn't agree with me. Morning sickness, upset stomach, severe headaches, extreme fatigue. For a while I couldn't play with the band. I was a little disappointed when they went on without me. The boys were always telling me how essential I was to their sound. I thought I was indispensable. Now I learned that I wasn't. There were no cross words. I never said a thing to Willie, Bud, or Dad. I kept my feelings to myself. But I secretly hoped the band might take a break.

The minute my health improved, I was back onstage, performing well into my eighth month. That helped boost my self-esteem. Since joining Bud Fletcher and the Texans, I was no longer welcome on the revival circuit. My only musical outlet was the band I'd helped form.

I bought into Bud's vision that someday we'd hit it big. He saw us moving on from Waco to Dallas to Houston and winding up in Nashville. He envisioned us on the *Grand Ole Opry.*

The thing I didn't see was that, although I was overjoyed at the prospect of becoming a mother, starting a family with Bud would, like my parents' marriage, end in catastrophe. Between 1950 and 1953, I'd give birth to three sons. The idea that those children would be ripped from my arms was absolutely unimaginable. Even now I struggle to tell that story.

I've never told the story before.

BROTHER

In 1951, the year after Bud and Bobbie had their first son, Randy, I was eighteen years old and, seeing I was about to be drafted, enlisted in the air force. That ended my stint with Bud Fletcher and the Texans. It'd been great, and I still credit Bud for believing in me. And I still credit Bobbie for covering up my bad notes—and, believe me, there were many. But now there were different romantic dreams dancing through my head. The Korean War was ablaze, and I dreamt of going over there as a fighter pilot. I also dreamt of playing new kinds of music.

Before boot camp in San Antone, I'd discovered Django Reinhardt, the Romani guitarist who grew up in Belgium. No other musician has had a greater influence on me. Some local guys who fought in World War II in France, where Django gained his fame, brought back his records. They knocked me clean off my feet. He had a style all his own. It was swing, it was jazz, but it was also something I'd never heard before. I felt like his guitar was talking to me. Django filled every song he played—even sad songs—with pure joy. His songs were like little short stories.

Then when I heard Django's personal story, he became like a folk hero to me. At eighteen, he was almost killed in a caravan fire. His legs were burned so badly he was told one had to be amputated. He refused. Two of the fingers on his left hand also suffered severe burns to the point of paralysis. They told him he'd have to give up guitar. *Never,* he said. Not only did he keep playing, but he found a way to turn the handicap into an advantage. He reinvented his guitar by soloing with only two fingers. He got better.

I followed Django's fortunes. I read how Duke Ellington invited him to New York and how jazz stars as different as Louis Armstrong and Dizzy Gillespie praised him to the sky. When they asked him which camp he was in—traditional or modern—he said both. His main partner was Stéphane Grappelli, a fiddler. In country, guitars and fiddles go together like ham and eggs. Same was true in Django's sound. Musically, he and Grappelli talked to each other like old friends. That's the feeling I was always looking for. It reminded me of the musical rapport I had with Bobbie.

I knew that Django had absorbed many influences—ragtime, Dixieland, big bands, even bebop—and found a way to capture them all in his own style. He was the first instrumentalist who taught me what it means to have your own voice. After two notes, you knew it was Django. He taught me that every solo you take can be heartfelt and simple.

I had this fantasy that somehow the air force would land me in Paris and I'd get to meet Django. I got no farther than Mississippi. I learned real fast that the military and I didn't mix. Made it through basic training at Lackland in San Antone and, being a good athlete, got promoted right quick to first class. But then it took only twenty-four hours to lose that promotion 'cause I got into a little brawl with a superior. Then it was off to Sheppard in Wichita Falls, where I worked on my poker-playing skills before being shipped to Biloxi, where the math class did me in. I wound up in the shipping room lifting fifty-pound boxes that wrenched my back. After I spent two months in the medical ward, the doctor gave me a choice—major surgery or discharge.

I took the discharge.

SISTER

Willie joining the air force came as no surprise. Spontaneity is Brother's middle name. Willie was always making surprise moves. Yet for all those moves, he always found his way back home to those who knew and loved him best. Whatever else he might be, Willie's a family man.

My own family came to life in what seemed like a blinding flash. The flash contained both great joy and great pain.

The joy was in the births of Randy in 1950, Michael in 1952, and Freddy in 1953.

The pain was in the collapse of my marriage.

Seven decades later, I look back at myself as a young woman coming into her twenties. I was desperately in love with Bud—desperate in the belief that the strength of my love would save our relationship. I was playing by the rules of the fifties. Stick by your husband no matter what. I was also moved by the high regard both my brother and my dad had for Bud, and the assurance from his own parents, Deacon and Mrs. Fletcher, that their son would eventually straighten out.

I knew the problem. Everyone did. It was more than just drinking. It was alcoholism. Today they know it's a disease. Back then they said it was just "men being men." I tried my best to save him. I tried reasoning, but reason went out the window. He couldn't stop. I wanted to save him, not only for his own sake, but for the sake of our children. I felt inadequate because I didn't know how to save him. Crazy as it sounds, I found fault with myself. *A smarter and stronger woman*, I reasoned, *would find a way to stop this good man from destroying himself.*

I don't want to detail all the horrific episodes. They're easy to imagine. They involve irresponsibility, brutality, and mental illness. It hurts me to write those words, but I cannot tell the story and pretend it didn't happen. It did happen.

But I don't feel judgment or condemnation for a man who was ill and never received the right treatment. Maybe I do judge and condemn myself for not being smarter and getting out sooner. I felt trapped. But I was only trapped by my own lack of wisdom, lack of experience. I had the illusion that the birth of these precious boys, whom I adored, would somehow bring Bud to his senses. He loved them as deeply as I did. I foolishly felt that fatherly love would be enough to ultimately get Bud to stop drinking. I, of course, was wrong. But it was a nice dream.

In this same period, Willie experienced his own heartache. Released from the air force, Willie was back in Abbott living with Mama Nelson. That's when he fell in love with a woman named Mary. Their affair was secret. Mary had another man. Nonetheless, she became pregnant with Willie's child. She met a married couple who expressed interest in adoption. So immediately after giving birth to the baby girl, she gave the infant away. Then Mary disappeared.

My brother was devastated.

BROTHER

Losing Mary and the baby was a heavy blow. Didn't matter that I was young and foolish. I was in love. I wanted Mary. I wanted to be a dad to our child, but circumstances didn't allow it. Just as my dad and mom weren't ready to be parents when they had children, neither were me and Mary. And it was Mary's choice. She found a good home for the baby. And, because Mary had a boyfriend, our secret relationship stopped before it started. Sad situation. It would take a lifetime before I met my daughter. More on that later.

ZEKE VERNON WAS my best friend. We met when I was sixteen and he was twenty-two. He was one of the great characters in all Hill County, Texas. Everyone knew Zeke. The man was an institution. Like Bud Fletcher, Zeke was all about having fun. Like Bud, he'd been in the service. And also like Bud, he was a smoker, drinker, and world-class gambler. You played poker and dominoes with Zeke at your own risk. He took no prisoners.

First time I saw Zeke was at the Nite Owl, a barroom on the county line where Bud Fletcher and the Texans performed. He liked my singing and playing. Before Zeke, most of my fans were local high school girls. Along with Bud, Zeke was the first adult to see me as a serious artist with real potential. He became my biggest champion. And also my guide into the night life.

It'd be another decade before I wrote lyrics that said, "The night life . . . ain't no good life, but it's my life." During that decade, I learned a lot from Zeke about forging ahead into unknown territory. Zeke knew no fear. He ran a poker game out of a trailer in his hometown of Hillsboro. His underground bookie operation was notorious, the biggest in Hill County. And the minute it looked like the law might catch him, he'd hop a freight train. Sometimes I'd hop that train with him. He showed me how to live life on the run.

Zeke had me working with him in Tyler, 115 miles east of Abbott, trimming trees till I fell from a high limb and nearly broke my neck. Never did get angry at Zeke, though. He had a Zen-like thing about life. Take it as it comes. And take as much as you can while you're here.

It was Zeke who had me move to Waco. By then, Bud was in no shape to keep his band together and I found a few gigs of mine. Bobbie and I had won that talent contest on radio station WACO, so I had a good feeling about the city. WACO was also where Hank Thompson, then called Hank the Hired Hand, hit the airwaves and made a name for himself. Never will forget his first big record, "Whoa Sailor!" I also remember the time when Hank played the gym at Abbott High and had braces on his teeth. That was before he became a national star on the wings of his "Wild Side of Life," the song that said, "I didn't know God made honky-tonk angels." Love that line.

Those were the words I was thinking when Zeke and I pulled up to a burger joint where a carhop in a halter top and cutoff jeans came to take our order. She was a dark-haired beauty, a full-blooded Cherokee. Her eyes set my soul on fire.

It was 1952. I was nineteen and, like the B. B. King song says, she was sweet sixteen. Her name was Martha Jewel. In an instant, I couldn't imagine living life without this Indian princess.

It helped that she'd heard me play at some school dances. But it still took a whole lot of sweet-talking to get a date. Everything about Martha was hot—her temper, her body, her love of making love. I fell, she fell, and just like that we ran off to Cleburne, where we added two years to her age since you had to be eighteen to marry. We had nowhere to live and no money to speak of. What to do? Where to go?

"Come home," said Mama Nelson, the world's most welcoming woman.

So it was back to Abbott.

SISTER

Willie and I took turns leaning on Mama Nelson. I'd go home to Abbott whenever things with Bud got especially rough. Then I'd be back in Waco, where Bud's parents would pay our rent and give us a little breathing room. The year Willie married Martha—1952—was the same year I gave birth to our second son. These pregnancies, one after another, kept me home and committed to Bud, despite the fact that he could no longer hold a job and wasn't around all that much. Most of the time I didn't know where he was. He'd just flat disappear. Bud wasn't even there to discuss the name of our child. Willie was. "If I ever had a son," he said, "I'd name him Michael Wayne." Well, what was good enough for Brother was good enough for me. My beloved Michael Wayne was a hard delivery, so hard I wasn't sure I'd be able to have another child. But sure enough, fifteen months later I gave birth to Freddy, our third boy. A month earlier, in October 1953, Willie and Martha had their first child, Lana. By then they were living in San Antonio and were having their own marital problems.

I loved Martha and her free spirit—the strength of which matched my brother's—but that was the problem.

My own problem of raising three young boys without Bud around was solved by the presence of Mama Nelson. There's an expression that says, "A praying woman can save a whole household." Mama Nelson was that very woman. She not only prayed for my little family, she helped sustain us by making sure we had food on the table and a roof over our heads. If I was feeling down, she had me playing those old hymns on the piano, knowing that music always brought me up. Her can-do attitude was contagious. She led by example. She had survived the death of her husband, showing me that a woman can do it on her own. That was a lesson long in learning. And it became the central lesson of my life.

BROTHER

After marrying Martha, I was going every which way. I worked in a saddle factory doing heavy stitching but had to quit when my fingers started bleeding to where I couldn't play guitar. Meanwhile, Martha was working as a waitress. Pretty as she was, she always came home with good tips. Much as she loved and respected Mama Nelson, Martha wanted a place of our own. I couldn't blame her for not wanting to live in her mother-in-law's house in the tiny town of Abbott. Problem was, though, I couldn't afford a place of our own.

I wasn't getting much music action in Hill County. Dad had moved to Fort Worth, where he made a living as a mechanic, not a fiddler, and couldn't really help us out. So I thought of Mom. Hadn't seen her in years and missed her something awful. She'd moved to Eugene, Oregon. Meanwhile, Martha and I were fussin' and fightin' so bad we both figured a new place might do us good.

Hello, Eugene.

I liked it. Pretty scenery. Clean air. For a while, it worked out. Being two thousand miles away from home was exciting. Plus, Mom and Martha got on good. As women who weren't about to be dominated by men, they understood each other.

Just so happened that western swing was on the rise in the

Pacific Northwest. That led me to finding work in a country band that played on the *Hayloft Jamboree,* a radio show on station KUGN. Good as the gig was, it lasted only a few weeks. A plumber hired me as an assistant, but he soon saw that when it came to unclogging drains I wasn't worth a damn. That meant once again living on Martha's wages as a waitress. When she got tired of serving up burgers and fries, we both decided we'd had enough of Eugene. Time to kiss Mom goodbye and head back to Texas.

Waco seemed like the right spot because the G.I. Bill gave me money to attend Baylor University. Don't know what got me believing I could be a college man. I wound up majoring in dominoes. Only lasted a semester or two. By then we learned Martha was pregnant.

I was in Waco when the Great Tornado of 1953 came within fifty feet of wiping out Jim's Tavern, where I was sipping beer with my buddies. When we went outside to see what all the commotion was about, the Brazos River Bridge, right by the bar, had been reduced to rubble. Downtown Waco was wiped out. So were me and Martha.

Weather storms, marital storms, storms threatening total destruction. A lifetime later, my buddy Waylon Jennings would sing a song that says "Storms never last," but sometimes in my younger life I wasn't that sure. Seemed like the storms would never stop.

One good thing about a storm, though, is that it tends to wake you and shake you up and get you moving. After that Waco twister nearly pulled my head off, I knew it was time to get out of town. That's when we skipped out to San Antonio—bigger city, bigger possibilities—which was where our beautiful baby girl Lana was born.

PART III

THE STORY SADDENS...

SISTER

I wanted to erase the pain from my memory. For years I tried to block out the nightmare. I didn't want to go back and remember. It was a time when my world fell apart and I didn't see any way of putting it back together. I broke down and, were it not for Mama Nelson, I might never have gotten back up.

They took my babies away.

It happened in Abbott. It was 1954. Freddy, our third son, was nine months old. He'd just begun to walk. Michael was two. Randy was nearly four. I'd moved back home permanently with Mama Nelson because Bud could no longer provide for us. His parents had stopped helping out, and I couldn't pay the rent. Bud's drinking binges were more frequent. He couldn't function on any level—bandleader, husband, or father. When he did show up, I was frightened. He could be violent. That's why I left Waco. At the same time, I still desperately wanted to help him and continued to feel guilty that I lacked the means to do so. I was a wreck.

Mama Nelson housed and fed us and helped me find work as a music teacher. But it was hardly enough to live on. Meanwhile, Mr. Fletcher, Bud's dad, thought that I was going for a divorce. That wasn't true. Foolish as it seems now, I clung to

the hope that one day Bud would find help and we could reunite. Besides, even if I did want a divorce, which I did not, I
didn't have any money to hire an attorney.

Mr. Fletcher knew none of this. He didn't ask to speak to
me. He didn't try to assess my attitude about the marriage. He
could have calmly discussed the situation with me but never
did. I have no idea why he had no interest in reaching out to
me. Instead, he used the legal system to attack me. Not only
was Mr. Fletcher a deacon at his church and the county road
commissioner, but his nephew was the chief magistrate at the
Hill County Courthouse, that same august building where
Daddy Nelson had taken me when I was a girl to hear the
gospel concerts.

I had no warning, no indication of what Mr. Fletcher
might do. One morning officials turned up at Mama Nelson's
and presented me with legal papers that said my children
would be temporarily under the custody of their paternal
grandparents, Mr. and Mrs. Fletcher. A hearing would be
held at the Hill County Courthouse in four weeks to render a
final judgment. I was in a state of shock. I could barely speak.
When I finally got out a few words—"How can you take away
my children without any reason?"—I was told that the court
had determined that the boys were not being cared for properly and until I could prove my worthiness they would be
situated elsewhere.

I was hysterical while Mama Nelson remained calm. She
assured me that something could and would be done. I
wanted to believe her but couldn't stop sobbing. The whole
scene took me back to that awful day when my parents abandoned us and left Abbott. My world had collapsed. During
both traumas—when my mom and dad moved from Abbott

and when I faced the threat of losing my children—my grandmother kept me from falling apart.

Mama Nelson's home had never seemed emptier, but I knew I didn't have time to feel sorry for myself. I had to take action. I got on the interurban and went from town to town, knocking on the door of every last lawyer. I got nowhere. Either they understood that the odds were stacked against me—that Mr. Fletcher and his nephew controlled the legal procedures—or they wanted an exorbitant fee I couldn't pay. The day before the hearing, I pleaded my case before still another attorney, an impatient man in his seventies.

"Little girl," he said, "you better get ready because tomorrow you're going to lose your children and there's nothing anyone, even a smart lawyer like me, can do about it. Everyone in these parts knows that you don't stand a chance against the Fletchers."

But I still harbored hope. I couldn't give up. They were my children. Bud, my husband, the father of these boys, did not attend the hearing. I later learned his parents, not trusting him to show up sober, had sent him to Florida.

In the cold courtroom, Mr. and Mrs. Fletcher sat at a long table along with their attorney. I sat at an equally long table alone. My own father wasn't there. He and his wife, Lorraine, had no interest in helping me out or taking responsibility for the boys. Dad sided with the Fletchers. He never said why, and I was too hurt to ask.

In court, I was allowed to speak first. I talked about my music students. I explained that my typing ability would soon get me a job as a secretary. The judge asked me whether I knew stenography. When I said no, he snickered. "Secretaries need to know stenography," he said, "and you'll never get hired as a secretary. You have no real way of making a living, do you?"

I promised that I would provide. Surely he understood a mother's love for her children.

"Not when the mother plays saloons," he said. "Not when the mother smokes and drinks."

"But I don't smoke or drink," I told him.

He just looked at me.

The judge said I'd have to remarry or straighten out my life. But my life was already straight. I was a faithful wife. I had no boyfriends on the side. My only concern was my children. The judge yawned.

Then Mr. Fletcher's lawyer spoke. He said that the Fletchers had a large house, a large farm, and more than adequate means to provide for their grandchildren. He went over Mr. Fletcher's credentials as one of Hill County's most upstanding citizens. Then the attorney pointed to me. Today I remember his description of me as the worst kind of stereotyping. Women were made to be homemakers. Women weren't meant to make music. This sharp-tongued lawyer called me the kind of woman whose only means of earning a living was playing piano in honky-tonks. He referred to me as a harlot. I broke down in tears.

The judge had no time for tears. He quickly rendered his verdict. The decision, he said, was simple. I couldn't support my sons. The Fletchers could. He named them permanent custodians.

Next case.

Next day the sheriff came and snatched the boys out of my arms.

BROTHER

"This is your ol' cotton-pickin', snuff-dippin', tobacca-chewin', stump-jumpin', gravy-soppin', coffeepot-dodgin', dumplin'-eatin', frog-giggin' hillbilly from Hill County."

I was a deejay, and deejays needed handles. I got me a good one. I started off in San Antone in a band called the Mission City Playboys and wound up working on the air at KBOP, a station about thirty miles outside the city, owned by a chiropractor named Dr. Ben Parker. A good man, he saw I had the gift of gab. I liked the job 'cause I got to play everyone from Porter Wagoner to Nat Cole. Was also great being at the turntable at the birth of rock 'n' roll. Spinning songs like Bill Haley & His Comets' "Rock Around the Clock" made me feel mighty good about the future of music.

But I couldn't feel too good about the future of me and Martha. One night when I was sleeping, she tied me up with rope and battered me with a broom. I never laid a hand on her, but that doesn't mean she didn't have reason to wallop me. Fidelity was never one of my strong points. Our fussin' and fightin' got worse over time, but I was also resolved to find peace.

I read books like Norman Vincent Peale's *The Power of Positive Thinking* that really did change my thinking. Got me to thinking, in fact, that I could be more of a positive force by moving Martha, Lana, and me out of San Antone to Forth Worth. My dad had been living there for some time. Fort Worth was a good music town. The deal was sealed when I learned that Mama Nelson and Sister were moving there as well. I knew Bud had been in bad shape for a long while, and that his folks had made noise about getting custody of my nephews, Randy, Michael, and Freddy. But when I learned that it had actually happened, I was stunned. How do you take kids away from their mother, especially a mother as loving and caring as Bobbie? Part of the answer was that other than Bud himself, the Fletchers hated the Nelsons. They looked down on us. They thought their son had married beneath his station.

Because the Fletchers were so powerful in Hill County, I was happy to hear that Mama Nelson was taking Bobbie to Fort Worth. I said I'd meet them there. It was crisis time, and crisis time means family time.

SISTER

I was broken.

Imagine losing your three children in an instant and having your reputation completely and wrongly smeared in the process. And being powerless to do anything about it at all.

I couldn't make any decision for myself, so I let Mama Nelson help direct me. She said it was best to go to Fort Worth and live with her daughter, Aunt Rosa. Seeing my emotional condition, Mama Nelson was not about to let me out of her sight. She was coming with me. Aunt Rosa, who was ten years older than my dad, and her husband, Uncle Ernest, had two young children at home, but they took us in anyway. Ernest worked at the Convair airplane plant, where they built bombers. The pay was minimal. Their small house in the White Settlement section of the city could barely accommodate us. But no one complained. We were welcome to stay as long as we liked. That is family.

When I learned Willie was also moving to Fort Worth, my spirits picked up. Willie always said Fort Worth was a music town with lots of bands and lots of work. He said any music gig for him meant a gig for me. I explained, though, that I couldn't play in a barroom or nightclub. My aim was to get my kids back. The court had already taken me to task for being "a woman of the night playing piano in dens of iniquity." I couldn't work anywhere where liquor was served. I'd have to find another way.

That wasn't easy. I was a twenty-four-year-old woman with musical skills, but those skills were doing me no good. I respected my talent to entertain people, but the judge didn't. The judge would continue to use that against me. I thought back to when the judge had laughed at me when I said I didn't know stenography. The judge, who had derided me, was the last person in the world who wanted to give me good advice. And yet maybe I could turn a negative into a positive. These were the thoughts running through my mind.

My mind was also overwhelmed with grief. To get myself going, I was drinking coffee by the gallon. That only made things worse. I don't know the exact definition of a nervous breakdown, but I could hardly sleep. I was filled with anxiety. A dark cloud of depression hung over my head. Mama Nelson, Aunt Rosa, and especially Willie did all they could to encourage me. They said I had to move forward. But sometimes, even when you know what you have to do, you can't do it. Sometimes you can't move at all.

Maybe it was weeks, maybe months. I can't remember how long I fell into a state of despair. At some point, though, I knew I couldn't stay down for much longer. I kept going back to the judge's accusation that I wasn't able to make a respectable living. Kept hearing the Fletchers' lawyer calling me nothing but a honky-tonk piano player. Kept thinking of my three boys living in Vaughan without their mom.

Then one day, something clicked. I want to say it was the spirit of God that got me going. A God who says *I'm not going to do for you what you can do for yourself.* A God that says *I'm here to love you, but you gotta make your own way through the world.* Doesn't matter if you're a woman or a man, rich or poor. You gotta deal with reality.

Deal with reality, Bobbie. You have no money, no car, no driver's license, but you do have energy. Use it. Get out of the house. Get any kind of job and use that money for business school. Business school is where you can improve your typing and learn to take dictation and how to run an office. You were always good at school. You like learning. God gave you a good brain. Apply it. Be practical. Get to work.

I went to the city employment office to get help finding a job. It took a while, but they found something. I became a receptionist at a TV repair shop, answering the phone and doing bookkeeping. The job was good except for the location. The shop was in a scary part of town. A group of mean-looking men, who loved leering at women, loitered right across the street. Seeing my unease, the shop owner, a good guy, walked me to the bus stop. But I was still on edge. At the same time, I was still determined. I used my small salary to enroll at the Brantley-Draughon Business College, where I learned stenography. Work during the day. Attend school at night.

Keep going.

Keep moving forward.

BROTHER

Sister is one strong woman. Sometimes she calls herself frail, and even though it might have looked like she was going to lose it, she loved her boys and, one way or the other, she was gonna get 'em back. Being dead broke is a lot different than being dead. We were all broke, all of us scuffling to get food for our family. But we were also blessed with that steely-strong Nelson sense of survival. To get by, you do what you gotta do. Bobbie was a lot more soft-spoken than our dad, mom, and me. She was gentle and vulnerable and, unlike me, not pushy. I believe Sister's soul is pure. But that doesn't mean she wasn't persistent. Besides that, she was the most naturally talented of all the Nelsons.

That's why I wanted her to join me when I played gigs out there on Jacksboro Highway. I knew she'd make me sound better. I also knew she could out-honky-tonk any honky-tonk piano player in town. But when she refused because it might hurt her court case, I didn't argue. I didn't want anything to get in the way of getting her boys back. Fort Worth night spots were rough. There could be knife fights, foul play, and police raids. Fort Worth was where the Wild West began, a wide-open town famous for whorehouses, back-room poker, and gun-slinging saloons.

Fort Worth was also where I met Oliver English. He was a

man who loved Django Reinhardt as much as I did and introduced me to the work of classical guitarists like Andrés Segovia. Oliver also introduced me to his brother Paul English, a genuine gun-totin' outlaw who turned into a first-class drummer plus my lifelong buddy. Not to mention lifelong protector. Famous for wearing black hats and capes that gave him a devilish demeanor, Paul would save my sorry ass more times than I care to count.

SISTER

Getting through every day was a challenge without my kids. But something happened during this period in Fort Worth that warmed my heart. Willie got on the radio. He was hired as a deejay on KCNC. Willie was wonderful on the radio because he never put on airs. He was always his natural self. While working at the TV repair shop, I'd have the radio tuned to his afternoon show, *Western Express.* Every day he'd play this song recorded by Guitar Boogie called "Red-headed Stranger" and dedicate it to his daughter Lana. I was so proud of my brother. Not only did he have a personality that could win over listeners, but he took the time to embrace his baby girl. The song, about a troubled cowboy, also spoke to me when it said, "He's wild in his sorrow, he's riding and hiding his pain."

I felt like I was doing the same. The pain of being separated from my boys never left me. I didn't get to cook them their dinner. I couldn't put them to bed, snuggle next to them and tell them stories. I didn't get to wake them up in the morning and greet their smiling faces with a kiss. I went about doing what I had to do: working at the repair shop, attending night school, trying to maintain positive thoughts. At the end of the day, though, my babies came to mind. All I could do was cry myself to sleep.

Willie inspired me because his get-up-and-go never stopped. He figured out how to do remote broadcasts of his radio show from places like Leonard's, the biggest department store in town. If a new car dealership opened or the circus came to town, Willie was there spinning records. He never missed a chance to promote his show. Although Bud was out of my life, I thought of him when I saw how Willie was pursuing his career with such enthusiasm. That's something he learned from Bud. Bud's drinking dampened his enthusiasm—his drinking drained away so many of his wonderful qualities—but I do believe that when it came to promotion, he influenced Willie in a positive way.

There's something else about my brother that not everyone knows. Every Sunday he went to the Metropolitan Baptist Church, where our dad and his wife, Lorraine, were members, and taught Bible class. It was no accident that, a little later, Willie would write his first hit song, "Family Bible." Willie knew the Good Book and the importance of its wisdom in our lives. Brother was grounded in God.

BROTHER

In the midfifties, Dallas–Fort Worth was alive with all sorts of good music. I wanted to play all of it. Wanted to be everywhere at once. I went to the Longhorn Ballroom and saw blues singers I loved, like B. B. King. Went to the *Big D Jamboree* broadcast, held in a wrestling arena, and heard Carl Perkins sing "Blue Suede Shoes" and Gene Vincent beat out his "Be-Bop-a-Lula."

I dreamt of playing in front of huge crowds but was grateful for the few party people who turned up at Gray's Bar, where I was performing with a Mexican band that had me singing jazz songs like "Sweet Georgia Brown." On some nights, I got even happier when black musicians turned up and jammed with us. They brought spontaneity and technical expertise that raised the musical level. I learned to go with the flow, and the more the musical flow was mixed, the more beautiful it became.

I also found beauty in faith. I loved teaching Sunday school because the students taught me as much as I taught them. They always had great questions about God. If you can't see God or hear God, how do you know he's real? My answer was usually something like . . . Well, you can feel him. You can also see him in your mother's eyes and hear him in your father's voice. That's if you have a loving mommy and daddy. I tried my best to be a loving daddy and a decent teacher. I taught that faith is a foundation to life. It's the anchor that keeps us connected to God. The simplest and best definition I know is that God is love, and if your foundation is love you're always standing on solid ground.

All was going well until the preacher at the church started asking me questions.

"What kind of work do you do?" he said.

"I'm a singer, guitarist, and writer."

"What kind of singing? What kinds of songs?"

"The kind that come from the heart," I said.

"Do you sing in barrooms?"

"Yes."

"Do people dance to your music?"

"Yes. Why are you asking me these questions now and not a couple weeks ago, when you baptized me?"

"That's different. I'm always impressed when an adult wants to be baptized. It shows you were interested in deepening your faith."

"I am," I said.

"Then why are you playing honky-tonks?"

"Because I like honky-tonks. Just like the church is your sanctuary, the honky-tonk is mine."

The preacher didn't like that at all.

"Good things happen in church," he said. "Bad things happen in honky-tonks."

"Well, the opposite might be true," I said. "While dancing in a honky-tonk, people might be thinking loving thoughts. While sitting in church, people might be thinking sinful thoughts."

He looked at me hard.

"Do you think God frequents honky-tonks?" he asked.

"I am sure he does. God is everywhere and everything, right?"

Preacher got fed up and came right to the point.

"Quit honky-tonks or quit teaching Sunday school."

I quit teaching Sunday school.

SISTER

Sundays always had me on edge. Those were the days the Fletchers allowed me to see my babies. All week I looked forward to the visit. But the visits themselves weren't easy. I borrowed a friend's car to drive from Fort Worth to Vaughan. That made me nervous because I didn't even have a driver's license. I'd learned on Bud's pickup truck but was never good at it. It was raining one Sunday, and I drove slowly. On the way there, my mind was racing. I was always nervous. I knew the boys would be overjoyed to see me, and I'd soon have them in my arms, but I also knew that I wasn't wanted. The Fletchers allowed me to visit because their conscience forced them to do so. It was enough to take children from their mother. Not allowing the mother to see those children was too much. At the same, they never invited me into the house itself and I never knocked on the door. If it was a rainy day, the boys and I visited in the car.

By the time I arrived that day, the rain had stopped and the sun had broken through. Randy, Michael, and Freddy were waiting for me on the porch. The minute I drove up, they ran to the car and were all over me, fighting to see who could kiss me first. They took turns sitting in my lap. I sang to them. I told them stories. I brought crayons and coloring books. Sometimes I brought little toy cars and trains. We walked around the farm. They liked watching the pigs slosh around the pen. They ran after the chickens and played hide-and-seek. We were all happy until the sun began setting and I knew it was time to leave my children behind. There was always a scene.

"Don't leave, Mama," Randy insisted.

"Stay with us," Michael cried.

"I don't want you to go," said Freddy.

Randy wanted me to hurry inside and convince Mr. and Mrs. Fletcher to let them come with me. They didn't understand why they couldn't live with me and Mama Nelson in Fort Worth. The crying, the clutching, the pleading went on and on. If it went on too long, Mr. Fletcher would come to the door and call the boys inside. He wouldn't look at me. I wouldn't look at him. I drove off and, as day turned to night, tears streaked down my cheeks. I was spent. I was miserable.

My misery was compounded by another fact. When I went to work in the mornings and school in the evenings, I saw a man following me. This became even more obvious after I started going out with a few guys. My dates were infrequent and never romantic. I did it mostly to avoid boredom. I also held a faint hope that maybe I'd meet someone who'd sweep me off my feet. That never happened. But something else did happen. While I was at dinner or a movie, spending time with someone I really wasn't interested in, both he and I noticed this same guy lurking behind us.

I later learned that the Fletchers were keeping tabs on me. They feared I would take legal actions and divorce Bud. If I did divorce Bud, that would mean he'd have to pay me alimony. As I understand alcoholism, it's progressive, and Bud was getting worse. He couldn't hold down a job. If he was court-ordered to pay alimony, his parents would have to foot the bill. And Mr. Fletcher, who not only didn't want to give me my boys, didn't want to give me a dime. He reasoned that if he could find dirt on me, he'd have leverage and force me to give up my plan to divorce their son.

Truth is, I had no such plan. Divorce was the last thing on my mind. I had no interest in squeezing money out of Bud. I was content to make my own money. I just wanted to attain enough financial stability to return to that scary Hill County Courthouse and prove to the judge that I had the means to care for my boys.

Then fate intervened. Doesn't it always? Taking the bus from White Settlement to the TV repair shop, I met a friendly woman my age. We often rode the route together. Her boyfriend worked for the phone company. He had a friend named Paul Tracy. Was I interested in meeting Paul? At first I wasn't sure. My few dates had been lackluster. But Mama Nelson and Aunt Rosa encouraged me to keep trying. I didn't have to go out on a date. I could just have him pick me up after work and drive me home.

Paul was a nice-looking man who, from the start, never hid the fact that he was smitten by me. Given my emotional condition, that was flattering. I was down on myself, and to have a man shower me with compliments boosted my spirits. He was also honest. He told me he was getting over a drinking problem. That alarmed me. It made me think of Bud, obviously. But Paul assured me that he only had an occasional beer. I told him that I couldn't go to places where beer was served. I didn't want the Fletcher spies photographing me in a bar. That's how determined I was to get my children back. Paul acquiesced. Paul was really in love with me. He took me to lavish dinners at fancy restaurants where liquor wasn't served. No man had done that before, not even Bud.

But here's the funny part. Here's the crazy part. I never stopped loving Bud. Part of me—a big part—wanted to get back with Bud. Part of me envisioned the reconciliation of our little family, me as Mommy, Bud as Daddy, Randy, Michael, and Freddy as our loving sons, all living happily ever after. I know that's ridiculous. And in the sane section of my mind I understood that would never happen. But true love isn't sane. It defies logic. I harbored this insane idea that Bud would regain his sanity. He never did. Yet it took me another two years to give up that hope. As I kept working at the repair shop, even as I graduated from business school and mastered the skill of stenography, I couldn't give up the dream that my husband would reform and our family reunite. Paul kept hanging around and taking me out, but, in my mind, strange as it was, Bud was still my man.

BROTHER

Fort Worth got to me. My deejay job dried up. The gigs on Jacksboro Highway were fewer and fewer. Cowtown had me down. Martha was feeling the same, so it took no convincing for her to agree to move to San Diego. I liked the idea of Southern California, mainly 'cause I'd never been there. I knew that the big San Diego navy base meant lots of clubs where servicemen could let off steam. As usual, Martha found work as a waitress while I scoured the scene looking for deejay gigs or a band in need of a singer/guitarist. Came up with nothing. That led to L.A. I promised Martha that as soon as I came with up a job, I'd send for her and Lana. But L.A. was even worse than San Diego. Couldn't even find work as a dishwasher much less a musician. Wallowing in despair, I decided to do what many men do when it seems like their world's falling part. I went to see my mother.

By then Mom was living in Portland. I bummed my way up there in a boxcar that took me as far as Eugene. A friendly trucker took me the rest of the way, where Mom's new husband, Ken "Kilowatt" Harvey, picked me up. You might have guessed that Ken was an electrician. When we arrived at the house, I was glad to see Mom, but shocked to see Martha and little Lana. I'd left them back in San Diego and hadn't even told Martha that I was going to Oregon. But Martha knew me as well as I knew myself.

"I knew where you were heading," she said. "I always know."

Martha had called Mom, who sent tickets for her and the baby. Well, that was fine with me. Fortunately, my wife forgave me for leaving her in the lurch. A little later we learned she was pregnant again. It was in Portland that our second beautiful daughter, Susie, was born at the start of 1957. I was twenty-three and even more desperate to find a way to make money making music. The second-best thing to making music was spinning records. So I convinced KVAN, 910 on your dial, a popular station serving the good folks of Portland/Vancouver, to put me on the air. The ad said, "Willie's got wit, warmth and wow . . . been entertaining folks since he was sweet 15 . . . and for the past 3½ years he's been a big name in Ft. Worth on station KCNC. But now he's moved 'kit 'n kaboodle' to Portland. And, ya know what? He likes rain!" It was all a lot of hype, but that's radio. Without hype, I'd be forgotten in a flash.

SISTER

Bobbie's sons—Randy, Michael, and Freddy—Fort Worth, 1961

My mother wrote about Willie's good fortune in Oregon, and of course I was happy for him. I also wasn't surprised. Brother always lands on his feet. I also couldn't wait to meet my new niece, Susie.

Meanwhile, Paul Tracy proved to be a steady force. He was bringing stability into my life, and that was a good thing. He couldn't have been more generous. He let me borrow his car to drive to Vaughan. He was always looking to buy me new clothes and trinkets. I was grateful, but new clothes and trinkets didn't matter to me. My children were all that mattered. I began thinking of a way that Paul might help me get my children back. He was strong. He was reliable. He made me feel protected at a time when I felt vulnerable.

My frustrations had been mounting. I had saved enough money from work to hire a lawyer in Waco who said he could help me regain custody. He had a good reputation and was respected by the legal establishment who ran the Hill County Courthouse.

"Your case is rock-solid," he told me. "You have a steady income. I see no reason why the court wouldn't give you custody of your children."

Hearing that, my heart sang with joy. But the joy didn't last long. A week later, I was called back to that same lawyer's office.

"I'm afraid I will be unable to take your case," said the attorney.

"I don't understand. Last week you said it was rock-solid. I gave you a deposit on your fee. In cash."

"I'm giving it back."

He handed me three crisp hundred-dollar bills.

"I don't want the money back," I said. "I want you to get me my boys."

"Perhaps another lawyer might—"

"Forgive me for interrupting, but by any chance did you speak to Deacon Fletcher?"

When the lawyer's eyes averted mine, I knew the answer. Bud's dad was intent on blocking me at every turn.

My heart stopped singing. It took a while to get over the disappointment, but I kept moving forward. I figured education was my main hope. That turned out to be true. The minute I graduated from Brantley-Draughon Business College, I went back to the city employment bureau to see if my new degree could help me get a better job. They directed me to the Shield Company, a huge store that sold a large variety of products, including major appliances. The beautiful thing— the thing that changed the course of my professional career— was that they had a department devoted to Hammond pianos and organs.

In the midfifties, the Hammond B3, their newest product, had proven extremely popular. From church organists to jazz musicians, everyone loved the Hammond B3 and the accompanying Leslie speaker that amplified its sound. It wasn't an easy instrument. Its complex keyboards, stops, and pedal configurations required skill. Some see it as the prototype to the synthesizer. It can create any number of voices. The Hammond B3 has a singing quality that creates an immediate emotional impact. It's a beautiful instrument.

My first job at Shield was to work as a typist and stenographer in the organ department. But once they saw I was a musician myself, they let me loose on the Hammond B3. It was love at first sight. I learned it quickly. In no time I was given a promotion and raise. I was teaching other musicians how to play this new organ as well as giving demonstrations to customers. Nothing could have made me happier—except, of course, getting my boys back.

To that end, my increased income allowed me to rent a small house on the south side of Fort Worth. Mama Nelson and I shared one bedroom, and my hope was that my children would share the other.

Things progressed slowly. I continued to borrow Paul's car to visit the boys on Sundays. My approach stayed the same. I never entered the Fletcher house. Randy, Michael, Freddy, and I remained outside. I was respectful. I kept my distance. I also never said a bad word about the Fletchers to my boys. Children need grandparents nearly as much as they need parents. Children don't want to be confused. They don't want to see their relatives feuding. Mr. Fletcher had hurt me as badly as I'd ever been hurt, but I tried my best to understand why he did what he did. It was for his son. He loved his children as much as I loved mine. I believe he was misdirected, but deep down I knew he was a decent man who wanted the best for everyone. The way I saw it, having a son as sick as Bud—especially when the sickness took the form of crippling alcoholism—confused Mr. Fletcher. That confusion led him to do things he ordinarily would have never done.

Maybe it was my lack of vindictiveness that turned the tables. I'm not sure. All I know is that one day at the end of a Sunday visit Mr. Fletcher called me into the home. We sat in the parlor and he came right to the point.

"I know you have a job, Bobbie," he said.

"Yes, sir, I do."

"And I presume you've stopped spending time in bars."

He made it sound like I had a history of going to bars to party when, in truth, the only reason I'd ever gone to bars was to play music as a professional. I decided, though, this was no time to argue with him.

"That's right, Mr. Fletcher. No bars."

"And you've been able to rent a house of your own."

"I have."

"Well, that leads me to believe that the boys could spend a week with you in Fort Worth, providing your grandmother will be there to care for them while you're off working."

"She'll be with them every minute I'm away."

"Okay. Let's give it a try."

I couldn't even speak. All I could do was smile. This was what I'd been praying for. And it happened.

The boys rode back to Fort Worth with me and stayed the week. Mama Nelson shared my joy. She said that God had answered our prayers. I said that it was only just a week's visit, but she saw the future more clearly than I did. She knew that three rambunctious boys had proven to be too much for the Fletchers. The kids had worn them out. They had hired a woman to look after their grandchildren but were tired of paying the extra expense. The Fletchers were ready to concede.

Over the following months, the kids came to Fort Worth more frequently. Finally, when it was time to enroll Randy in school, Mr. Fletcher agreed that should happen in Fort Worth.

And just like that, I had my kids back. I went to my knees and thanked God.

I wondered whether Mr. Fletcher would return to the Hill County Courthouse to turn custody back over to me, but he never did. I thought about hiring a lawyer to make it all legal. But what would be the point? Even if I could find an attorney willing to go up against Bud's powerful father, the expense would be exorbitant and probably only open another can of worms. I decided to leave well enough alone. I figured that Mr. Fletcher had had enough. I was grateful that, in his own way, he had finally put the boys' well-being first. Mind you, I never hated Bud's father. When he took my children from me, I had a hard time forgiving him. But when he relented and the boys were back with me, I did forgive him. My heart was free of bitterness.

BROTHER

There was Shorty the Hired Hand, Cactus Ken, and Willie Nelson.

"We're the station that makes you laugh and feel good," the promos said.

In the Portland/Vancouver market, KVAN was all about deejay personalities, and the station manager thought I was quirky enough to fit in. My first time slot was in the afternoon. When the listeners liked me, I got switched to morning drive time. That was fine, except that I was competing with Arthur Godfrey's national radio program. Back then, Godfrey was a household name, but he didn't bury me entirely. I held my own. The station kept touting my Texas twang and amiable chatter.

I wasn't so sure about all that, but I did have a good time playing the hits of the day by Johnny Cash, Ray Price, Ferlin Husky, and of course the breakout artist who, in 1957, had begun his takeover of the musical universe. That was the year of Elvis's "Hound Dog" and "Heartbreak Hotel." I liked Elvis. What I heard was a white boy who loved black rhythm and blues. He had country in his voice—he had listened to Ernest Tubb and Jimmie Rodgers—and, at the same time, he was a rock 'n' roller. He proved to be everything to everyone. I took note how he merged all these genres together and still stayed true to himself. If you were any kind of musician, Elvis impressed and even inspired you. There wasn't any material Elvis was afraid of tackling. Like me, he loved gospel hymns. He also loved crooners like Bing Crosby, Billy Eckstine, and Frank Sinatra. I saw him as a strong, positive force in American music. The prudes who said he was too sexy . . . Well, who cares what the prudes say?

In addition to learning from the artists I played on my show, I was also learning from my fellow deejays. At KVAN you needed to get out from behind the turntable and make a splash in public. I did that by riding a palomino and parading down Main Street. I went to the grand openings of supermarkets dressed as Davy Crockett. I rode in stock car races.

Deejaying was one thing, songwriting another. Never stopped writing. One thing in particular—a tune called "No Place for Me" that I'd recorded in Portland—was good enough for Starday, a label out of Houston, to release. Not a huge seller, but it made a little noise in Texas.

In Oregon, Mae Axton came to the station. She worked for Elvis's manager, Colonel Parker, who became one of the most powerful men in the music business. Mrs. Axton was in the Northwest promoting a Hank Snow tour. I knew her as the co-writer of "Heartbreak Hotel." She had a reputation as an influential lady in the music business. (Her son grew up to become the famous Hoyt Axton.) I'd just written another song that I thought had a wider appeal than "No Place for Me." It was sentimental but sincere. I called it "Family Bible." I based it on my memory of how Mama and Daddy Nelson kept our family Bible in plain sight at all times. They knew the Good Book and made sure its loving messages got through to their grandchildren. I recorded a rough version and convinced Mrs. Axton to give it a listen. She liked it.

"You got a gift, Willie," she said, "but it's being wasted up here. Why not go back to Texas?"

I had no real answer.

"Better yet," she said. "Go to Nashville. All the top song-writers are in Nashville."

"Not sure I'm ready for Nashville," I said, "but going home to Texas always sounds good."

The idea of Texas had taken an additional positive turn when Bobbie called to say she'd gotten her kids back from the Fletchers. I knew what those boys meant to her and the hell she had gone through when they were taken away.

Martha was ready to go back home as well. So we bundled up Lana and Susie, kissed my mom goodbye, and hit the highway.

SISTER

When Willie, Martha, and their babies returned to Fort Worth, they moved in with our dad, who was then working steadily as a car mechanic. I was so glad to see my brother and grateful that he was finally getting to bond with his nephews. From then on, Willie would be a wonderfully caring uncle to Randy, Michael, and Freddy.

Getting my boys back changed everything. We'd been apart far too long. Just being able to tuck them into bed at night had me in tears.

The first week they were with me, I joined the Edge Park Methodist Church, which was temporarily housed in a school building. We attended that church for years. Eventually Edge Park had its own small sanctuary, where I became the pianist. You can imagine the satisfaction of watching my three sons sitting on the first pew next to Mama Nelson as I played those old hymns—the same hymns that Mama Nelson had taught me back in Abbott.

Willie, being Willie, always found work in one band or another. He kept urging me to join in. I wanted to. Nothing gave me more pleasure than playing piano behind Brother's guitar and singing. But I had to say no because I was still paranoid about the Fletchers. Yes, they had given up the boys, and yes, I had custody, but I still had no legal documents. Besides, the trauma of all I'd gone through still lived inside me. I didn't want to take a chance of some legal eagle catching me playing in a honky-tonk and starting a court case all over again.

Things got even more complicated when, out of nowhere, Bud Fletcher called. We hadn't spoken for over a year. He said he'd cleaned up. He'd gotten a steady job with the Central Freight Lines. He had his own place, apart from his parents, and was finally ready to ask me something he'd been wanting to ask for a long time. Would I divorce him? His question shocked me, and my answer shocked me even more. I said no. I wanted us back together. Given his violent history, that was a crazy statement for me to make. But I'm here to tell you that I made it. I still wasn't ready to break out of whatever prison women find themselves in—especially women abused by men. I know there are whole books written about women who keep going back to men who are wrong and even dangerous. I was one of those women. I can also say that, at least in my case, I felt a love for this particular man that simply would not die. I was willing to take him back. He was the father of my boys. Surely there are other psychological reasons behind my willingness. Maybe those reasons have to do with a lack of self-esteem. But I don't know—my musical skills had rewarded me with strong self-esteem. I had confidence. So there are probably other reasons why I kept clinging to the hope of reconciling with Bud. Even if I could identify those reasons, they likely wouldn't make sense, because romantic love doesn't make sense.

Fortunately, Bud had better sense than me—at least in this instance. He insisted on the divorce, claiming he'd gotten a woman pregnant and needed to marry her. That turned out to be a lie, but at the time I believed him. I took the news hard. Mama Nelson took the news in stride and urged me to do the sensible thing—grant this man a divorce and get him out of my life. But in doing so, would I endanger my custody of the kids? Again, Mama Nelson, with her country wisdom, saw the situation for what it was. The Fletchers had tired of the children and weren't about to take them back.

The Bobbie Nelson/Bud Fletcher legal relationship officially ended when I signed that divorce decree toward the end of the fifties. We'd have one more encounter, but that wouldn't be for years. Meanwhile, foolish as it might seem, I mourned the end of a marriage to a man I hadn't seen in years yet loved like no other.

Paul Tracy stepped into the void. Now he couldn't wait to marry me. He was willing to take financial responsibility for everyone. He bought a house much bigger than the one I was renting. Mama Nelson would have her own room. The boys would be more comfortable. Paul had enough money to buy his own gas station. He was absolutely insistent on having me. He never tired of telling me how much he loved me. When I couldn't reply in kind, that didn't bother him. Finally, he wore me down. I took his hand in marriage. And even though I tried mightily, I never did find the love for him that every man deserves from his wife. I was weary of being alone and chose comfort over true romance. I didn't feel great about the choice, but I made it anyway. Adding to my guilt was the fact that Paul proved true to his word. He was a man I should have loved. I tried to convince myself to look at all the facts: He was a good provider; a good father to Randy, Michael, and Freddy; and someone eager to help out anyone in my family.

That included Willie.

BROTHER

The second time around, Fort Worth was just as rough as the first.

Gigs were few and far between. That's why I was mighty grateful when Bobbie's new husband, Paul Tracy, hired me at his station to pump gas and change oil. Didn't mind that kind of work, especially because Paul paid fairly. He was so stuck on Bobbie that he was determined to fit in and do right by the Nelson clan.

I shouldn't have been amazed to learn that, since I'd been gone, Sister had learned the Hammond B3 to where she was out there at car shows and conventions. I got to watch her demonstrate the instrument on a revolving stage. The way she'd mastered that organ made me proud. One minute she was playing "Stars and Stripes Forever," the next minute "The Yellow Rose of Texas." The B3 ain't for amateurs. You're working your hands and feet at the same time. Well, sir, Bobbie floated over those keyboards like a surfer riding waves. Sister knew how to maximize the instrument so it sounded like a sixty-piece orchestra.

I pleaded with her to sit in with some of the bands where I was playing. I could hear how perfectly her B3 would add to my guitar and singing. Plus, I wanted to feature her on as many songs as she wanted. And because she played by ear, she

knew virtually every song on the radio, going back to the forties when we first started loving the old standards sung by
Sinatra and Crosby.

"Wish I could, Willie," she said. "There's nothing I'd like
better. But I've got to stay out of the barrooms. I'm not doing
anything to risk losing the boys."

"Not sure you ever have to worry about the Fletchers
again. They're plumb tired of chasing after three youngsters."

"Probably, but I can't take any chances."

So I backed off. Bobbie was right to be extra cautious. Getting your children back after losing them will change the way
you think about everything.

Since I wasn't making a lot of money as a musician and
since Paul couldn't pay me enough to cover rent for me, Martha, and the girls, I had to change my approach. That was especially true when, in May of 1958, we had our third child and
our first son, Willie Hugh Nelson, Jr., whom everyone started
calling Billy. Loved him, just as I've loved all my kids, but
having him added to the financial pressure. With three kids,
Martha couldn't really work as a waitress. That meant I was
the money man.

I tried everything, including selling encyclopedias. Turned
out I was a crackerjack salesman.

"I have something to offer you that's more precious than
gold, but something you can afford," I'd say to the couple
who opened the door.

They looked a little perplexed.

"May I come in? I'll need only a few minutes of your time."

My approach was gentle but firm. When they asked what's
more precious than gold, my answer was, "Knowledge."

"I see you have two beautiful children," I'd say, "and I
know you want the best for them. You want them to go far in

life. Well, nothing will take them further than education. And education is something that comes from curiosity. Having this set of encyclopedias in your home will spur their curiosity—and your own curiosity as well. It's something I consider essential for a growing family. Curious about American history? There are hundreds of pages dedicated to that very subject written in language that's easy to understand and beautifully illustrated. Curious about religion? We all are. We're all curious about science and music and sports. It's like having an entire library of your very own. It's a way to enrich your lives and the lives of your precious kids."

My first day out I sold $400 worth of *Encyclopaedia Britannica*s. The only problem was getting hit by a big wave of guilt. Folks I was selling to were living in bare-bones apartments. Many were scraping by with hardly any food in the fridge. Then here comes this slick-talking Willie saying that, for only the daily price of a pack of Camels, the whole world of knowledge would open up to them. I was so good at turning this trick I made myself sick. So I quit.

Next up were Kirby vacuum cleaners. They were the top of the line. That meant my clientele had more money. I had less guilt, but it still wasn't much fun. I genuinely love people and most people genuinely take to me. That meant that I could sell about anything, but I didn't like the way it made me feel. I kicked the Kirbys to the side.

Paul Tracy's gas station was at least honest work and gave me time to go to the Fort Worth Public Library. I guess you'd have to say I took up the inexact art of self-education. Having dumped college for dominoes, I felt the need to feed my intellect. I checked out all kinds of books. I was especially interested in religion and how different cultures had different viewpoints on God. Read about Buddhism. Read about Juda-

ism and Hinduism. Even read up on pagan religions in an-
cient Greece. When it came to Christianity, my natural bent,
I started seeing that not all scholars read the Bible literally.
That was a revelation in and of itself. The Bible, because it's so
complex, requires interpretation. Also turns out there are
different gospels other than the ones I was taught as a child.
The Aquarian Gospel of Jesus the Christ, written by Levi Dowling in
the early twentieth century, fascinated me 'cause it said the
Lord went a-traveling. Said he ventured into India and beyond to absorb some of that mystical wisdom of the East. Also
said he fell for a lady but resisted the temptation of the flesh
to preserve all his divine energy. Most fascinating of all, the
book argued that Jesus came to believe in reincarnation. That
changed my whole outlook.

If Jesus believed that, why shouldn't I? After all, Jesus was
a perfect man. But for the rest of us who ain't perfect, we
need to keep coming back until we get it right. As a young
man, I knew I was doing okay spiritually, but I also knew I
wasn't close to getting it right. Reincarnation gave me hope.
It said it takes as long as it takes. I liked that notion.

SISTER

Promotion photo for the Hammond organ, 1963

While Willie was over at the library reading all these books on philosophy and religion, I was getting a different kind of education at Hammond, where responsibilities grew with every passing day. I became the private secretary to the manager. That meant taking dictation and handling his correspondence. Those were the days when many women like me actually ran whole operations but were still being called secretaries. We weren't given credit for our accomplishments and, compared to our male counterparts, were woefully underpaid. Yet that wasn't my mindset. I was happy to have a job. Happy to be a workingwoman. Happy to gain independence.

My boss also put me in charge of the sheet music department. In the fifties, sheet music was still an important business. It sold in great numbers and usually featured a fancy illustration or photograph. Whether it was Johann Strauss's favorite waltzes or Hoagy Carmichael's "Rockin' Chair," Hammond carried it. My job was to organize the sheet music into genres before alphabetizing them by composer. Beyond that, a customer might ask me to play the composition. I was always delighted to do so. I was always happy to give a customer an on-the-spot lesson.

Teaching was rewarding, but performing was even more satisfying. Hammond taught me to combine performing and selling. I'd never be as good a salesman as Willie. People naturally believe anything Willie says. He just has that thing. But I wasn't half-bad either. Hammond would set me up, for instance, in the middle of the Fort Worth Coliseum. Anything might be going on—a stock car show, a rodeo, an auto parts convention. I'd sit at the Hammond B3 on a little stage with my own microphone. "I can show you how to play this instrument," I'd say. "It's easy. It's fun. Anyone can learn. Including you." Then I'd start playing a popular number of the day like "True Love," the song Bing Crosby sings to Grace Kelly in the film *High Society*. Folks would flock over. A little girl might climb onstage and sit on my lap and let me put her hands on the keyboard. I loved the expression on her face when she heard the soaring sounds emanating from that fabulous organ.

Those big convention centers were exciting, but I was just as happy to do a demonstration at a supermarket or in a Pontiac showroom. The truth is that I was a good saleslady because I really believed in the product. I loved the product. The Hammond B3 became my friend. I saw it as a lifesaver.

And what was doubly beautiful about its emergence as a popular instrument was that churches were adopting it with as much enthusiasm as nightclubs. Its flexibility was astounding. Playing a hymn on the B3 made the hymn sound fuller. Playing a love ballad made the song sound sexier. It was an innovation that, thanks to a wondrous coincidence, put me in the vanguard, not to mention in demand. I'd never been in that position before. With the boys thriving under the care of two women—Mama Nelson and myself—and a devoted stepdad, my life had unexpectedly moved in a positive direction. All I could do was keep playing and thank God.

BROTHER

I kept playing the honky-tonks but getting nowhere. Music was not paying the bills. In addition to pumping gas at Paul's gas station, I started working at a grain elevator. When I fell asleep at that job, I was fired and found something else—a laborer for a carpet removal service.

None of this was what you'd call fun. The only little breakthrough came with a band at the Cowtown Hoedown, a show taking place at a run-down downtown Fort Worth movie theater. I played guitar in the house band. The band wasn't good, the pay was lousy, but the featured artists were great. Got to see everyone from Faron Young to Roy Orbison.

The show's promoter was a character named Uncle Hank Craig, who thought I had some talent and, hearing about my deejay history, had me cut a commercial for XEG, a station in Mexico that was hustling aspiring songwriters. The deal was this: XEG would solicit listeners to send them their half-finished song. Then the station paid me to finish it, sing it, and send the disc to the aspiring songwriter. All for the bargain-basement price of ten bucks. At the same time I was working that side of the street, Uncle Hank had ministers selling bottles of holy water and baby chicks. I used to joke that he'd hawk autographed glossy photos of Jesus if he thought they'd sell.

Uncle Hank, who became my champion, worked it so I could cut a couple of my songs. The records came out but never went anywhere. It was Uncle Hank who encouraged me to get out of Fort Worth. He said I need something bigger. Houston was the biggest city in Texas.

Go to Houston.

PART IV

THE STORY TURNS TO SONG ...

SISTER

In trying to find his fortune, Brother was persistent. By "fortune" I don't mean money. I mean his desire to be able to live on his musical labor. The Hammond Organ Company allowed me to do just that. That was enough for me. I was satisfied with my work and grateful for getting paid to play. Yet Willie, whose musical vision was far greater than mine, was still struggling. That hurt my heart. But it also inspired me to see how he'd go to any lengths to keep writing and performing. When he went to Houston, it was probably the lowest point of his professional life. He didn't even have enough money to bring Martha and the babies. Mama Nelson and I did our best to help out.

It didn't seem that he was there that long. When he returned to Fort Worth, he came over to our house. Paul and Mama Nelson had taken the children out for dinner. I had a pile of sheet music I'd taken home to learn. We hugged, as we always did, before I asked Willie how Houston had treated him.

Not one to complain, Willie said it hadn't been easy but at least he'd been writing some pretty good songs and sold a couple. "Willie," I said, "that's wonderful." The songs had sold for only $200, but then he'd written a bunch more and, given how much he needed money, was willing to sell them for a lot less. Yet no one would buy them. One guy said he shouldn't sell them because one day they'd be worth thousands. Another guy said one of them should be recorded, with Willie doing the vocal. They went to Gold Star studios, where blues singer Lightnin' Hopkins had recorded. Willie sang the song, but the owner didn't like it 'cause he claimed it didn't sound country. It sounded like the blues. He pressed a few records anyway, but no one bought 'em, so Brother was pretty down.

I asked him if he could sing me the song. I was dying to hear what Willie had written. As he started to sing, I sat at my little spinet piano and, hearing the melody, was able to accompany him. The song was "Night Life."

"Willie," I said, "that song is beautiful. Everyone's going to love that song."

Because the words said that "the night life ain't no good life but it's my life," he thought the song might be too much about him—too autobiographical—for anyone to care. I said millions of people will relate to the story. I said he'd written a masterpiece.

I think my words encouraged him because he started singing other songs he'd written when he was down and out in Houston. I stayed at the piano and was able to augment his melodies. I don't mean that I added to them. They were already written. So were the lyrics. Willie sang them all with that aching beauty that is the hallmark of his voice.

One was about a couple meeting at a bar. They used to be lovers but she had moved on. The words said, "It's been so long now, seems it was only yesterday. Gee, ain't it funny how time slips away."

Another began by saying he was crazy, "crazy for feeling so lonely . . . crazy for feeling so blue . . . crazy for loving you."

Willie kept singing and I kept playing.

The third song was talking to Mr. Record Man. "I'm looking for a song I heard today. There was someone blue singing 'bout someone who just went away."

The fourth was a man drowning in his tears, so sad that all he could do was drink. "Gotta get drunk and I sure do dread it 'cause I know just what I'm gonna do—I'll start spending my money and calling everyone honey and wind up singing the blues."

The last song said, "Let's call it a night, the party's over. They say, 'All good things come to an end.'"

I said, "Willie, there's no end to the beautiful songs you've been writing. These are classics. People are going to be singing and playing them forever. How long did it take you write 'em all?"

"A week or two," he said.

I was stunned.

"That's amazing."

"They just started falling down on me like stars from the sky," he explained. He talked about how he'd found work at a place called the Esquire Ballroom. He'd also reunited with an old friend from Fort Worth named Paul Buskirk, a fine musician who'd set up a guitar school in Houston. Paul had always been a big believer in Brother. He was the one who warned Willie about selling these fabulous songs for next to nothing.

"These songs gotta get to the world," I kept saying.

I was so moved that I asked him to sing them all over again. Having heard them once, I had a better sense of how to accompany him as he sung.

"Night Life."

"Funny How Time Slips Away."

"Crazy."

"Mr. Record Man."

"I Gotta Get Drunk."

"The Party's Over."

When he got through singing them again, he looked over at me.

"You're crying," he said.

"You too."

His eyes were filled with tears.

We didn't have to say anything else. My brother had found a way to take his life experience and turn it into song. I'm not saying he was the real-life character of every song-story he wrote. Writers are inventive, and Willie invented people and scenarios based on whatever he had observed. But the inventions were based on reality. Everyone could relate to the emotions. They weren't fancy songs; they were true songs that came from the deepest part of his soul. I also knew that even Willie, who, for all his spunk, can underestimate himself, couldn't deny what he had done. Down there in Houston, as lonely as he was, as broke as he was, as tired as he was of chasing after gigs, he had nonetheless found his fortune. My brother had discovered that he was more than a good writer. He was a great writer. And knowing that, he had no choice but to point his whole life in a different direction.

BROTHER

Nashville scared me, just like it scared lots of writers. Last thing in the world I wanted was to be another one of those pickers who wind up working at some car wash. I knew Nashville was the ultimate place for country composers, and I knew my writing was getting better by the day, but I'd also been banging my head against the wall. I'd been struggling like the dickens to make some money at the music game and failed miserably. If I failed in Texas, why would Nashville be any different?

Fortunately, there were voices in my life that argued otherwise, principally Bobbie's. Because I respected her musicianship—and her honesty—when she said she was sure I'd make it in Nashville, I was inclined to believe her.

I had no doubt that the tunes I'd written in Houston were good. I was able to say things in song I hadn't been able to say before. I was more emotionally to the point. My language was more direct. Because some of those songs eventually turned into standards, I've been asked in dozens of interviews to describe my growth as a songwriter and describe my artistic process. My answer never satisfied the music journalists, but it's the only answer I can give:

I don't know.

I've never tracked my growth. I've never analyzed my

process, because I can't do it honestly. I've done what I've done when I've done it. Sure, I can go back and say I wrote lonely songs in Houston 'cause I was a lonely man. I can say I wrote drinking songs 'cause I was a drinker. I can say I wrote songs about being crazy in love 'cause I'm a man inclined to be crazy in love. But that's about all I can say, and it's obviously a lot more complicated than that.

Honest truth is just this: I write out of instinct. In every period of my life I've written some good songs and some not so good. I can't say why the good ones came when they did. But when they did come, all I could do was express gratitude to God. He's the creator. I'm the vessel. As time went on, though, I did see that I needed to pursue creativity more aggressively. I wanted more people to hear my songs, and I also wanted to make money.

That's why at the start of the sixties I got behind the wheel of my broken-down 1950 Buick and left Fort Worth. True to form, my first stop was in the wrong direction. I headed south to Waco to drop off Martha and the kids. My wife and I figured she'd better stay with her folks until I got settled in Nashville. We knew that could take a while.

Got to Nashville and ran into an old friend from Texas, Billy Walker, who put me up for a few months when I faced the age-old problem of how to scrape together a living. Once again, I couldn't make enough—either as a player or a writer—to cover the bills. If you can believe it, I was back out there pounding the pavement selling encyclopedias. Didn't like doing it in Tennessee any more than I liked doing it in Texas. But I needed to do something to get enough to send for Martha and the kids.

When they showed up, we lived in a trailer camp—$25 a week rent—until Martha wound up working as a manager at a joint called the Hitching Post while, on her off days, she waited tables at another joint called the Wagon Wheel.

God bless Martha.

In those early Nashville days, I can't say I was feeling any kind of blessing. I put in my time at Tootsies Orchid Lounge across from the Ryman Auditorium, home of the *Grand Ole Opry*. I met other songwriters like Hank Cochran (famous for writing "I Fall to Pieces" for Patsy Cline) and Roger Miller (famous for writing "Dang Me," "Chug-A-Lug," and "King of the Road"). They were encouraging, but encouragement wasn't buying me any beers. I was buying my booze with the money made by my wife. She remained the main earner. And that didn't make either of us happy. She and I were fighting worse than ever. I started drinking more than ever.

One time in the dead of winter I was so down on myself I lay down in the middle of the street half hoping a car would ride over me. No such luck. It wasn't going to be that easy. I had to get up off my ass and, like everyone else in this cold world, keep on trying to figure out how to make a living.

Like Sister, Hank Cochran was really moved by those songs I wrote in Houston. Without Hank, I'm not sure I would have gotten through this bout of the blues. Hank did more than tell me I was good; he said he wanted to write with me. Not only that, being among the best writer-hustlers in the business, Hank hustled us a deal with a song publisher outside of Nashville that paid me fifty bucks a week.

All thoughts of suicide vanished.

Fifty bucks sounded like a fortune.

SISTER

In 1961, less than a year after Willie got to Nashville, Bud Fletcher got into a near-fatal car accident. I wasn't with him, but, in a strange and unexpected way, that accident came close to destroying me.

Bud had been in many collisions, almost all due to his drinking. But I'd been led to believe he'd stopped drinking. He hadn't. His alcoholism remained untreated. He'd also developed a blood clot in his lungs. He was in bad shape. Then came this horrible wreck when he ran his brand-new pickup off the road that put him in the Veterans Hospital in Dallas.

He said he wanted to see me.

My husband, Paul, was kind enough to drive me there and leave the two of us alone. I was shocked to see Bud. The doctors had warned me that his head injury was severe. But I wasn't prepared. His face was ghostly pale and his breathing was labored. He was at death's door. I held back tears. I didn't want to alarm him. I held his hand.

He smiled and whispered, "Oh, Bobbie."

We looked into each other's eyes.

"You know, I always loved to hear you play the piano. You don't know the joy that brought me." I started crying.

I said something that I knew to be God's truth. "You know I still love you, Bud. I'll always love you."

He managed a smile. I could feel him trying to squeeze my hand, but he was too weak. We managed to carry on the conversation a little longer, but he was so frail I knew I had better leave. Soon after our visit he lost consciousness.

One month later he died.

His death greatly disturbed Randy, our oldest son, and greatly disturbed me. Whatever fury I had felt about having lost my boys to Bud's parents was gone. I had forgiven the Fletchers. I had forgiven the lawyers and the judge at the Hill County Courthouse, where those events had traumatized me. Maybe because Bud's death itself was a trauma, I fell into a deep and dark depression.

Even before his accident, I had been working too hard. I'd signed up over a dozen students and was giving Hammond B3 demonstrations in both Fort Worth and Dallas. I was performing on the instrument at schools and in churches. I was running the Hammond office, I was heading the sheet music sales, I was tending to my boys, I was getting little sleep, and, at the time, was unable to lift the weight of guilt on my heart—the guilt that said I had married a man I did not love. I grew dizzy, light-headed, and many times during the day had to sit down to avoid collapsing. Mama Nelson insisted that I go to the doctor, whose orders were clear. Take off time from work. But how could I? We needed the money. Health is more important than money, the physician said, before explaining the paradox: I have to stop working to eventually keep working.

I knew he was right, but my compulsion got the best of me. I took off some time but not enough. I went back to my grueling schedule. Another doctor had given me what must have been a primitive antidepressant. The drug made me feel even worse. Mama Nelson warned me to stop taking it, but I ignored her advice. I was hoping that the beneficial effects would soon kick in. They didn't. Instead I broke down completely. Both mentally and physically, I collapsed. I was rushed to a hospital, where a hysterectomy was performed. The details explained by the doctor remain fuzzy. But one thing was clear. After I was admitted because of mental problems, a thorough physical exam pointed to the urgent need to remove my uterus. Still groggy after the operation, I remember thinking, *Bud and I can have no more children.* When I realized Bud was dead, I relived that all over again. Even more startling, I looked up and saw that standing beside my bed was Paul, the loyal handsome husband whom I did not love.

I tried to take a deep breath.

I did not understand my life.

BROTHER

I was sitting in this little ol' office in Goodlettsville, Tennessee, where for the first time in my twenty-seven-year-old life I was paid to hang out nine to five and write songs. That was a strange position to be in. A good position 'cause it sure beat selling encyclopedias and pumping gas, but a pressure position 'cause never before had I been hired to write on command. I'm not that kind of writer.

Some folks can do that. Publisher says, "Write me a song," and the song gets written in an hour. That ain't me. I gotta wait for the spirit to bring the song to my heart and mind. That could happen in the middle of the night or while I'm taking the dog for a walk. Inspiration isn't something under my control.

Then there was the question of style. Those were the days of the Nashville Sound, the product of two talented men—Owen Bradley at Decca and Chet Atkins at RCA. These were both great musicians, Owens, a pianist, and Chet, one of the all-time great guitarists. But they made their mark as producers. The big hits were big productions. Remember Marty Robbins's "El Paso"? Or Ferlin Husky's "On the Wings of a Dove"? Lush strings, elaborate background harmonies, flutes and French horns, harps and heavy arrangements. It was bombastic.

I wasn't sure I could write in that style. Hank Cochran was there to assure me, though, that I didn't have to. "Just write what you wanna write," he'd say. But what *did* I wanna write? Me and Hank were stuck in that office, looking at each other like two fools without an idea between us. Then one afternoon Hank got bored and walked away for a while. I just looked around and, for no reason at all, said, "Hello, walls." That was a stupid phrase. What was I doing, talking to the walls? But the phrase stuck. I liked the way it sounded. I added, "How'd things go for you today?" Another stupid phrase, but it seemed to go with the first one. Could have quit right then, but I felt like I was onto something. I just needed a story. The story came with the third line, "Don't you miss her since she up and walked away?" Now I had something to go on. The woman that walked away is always a good story. Long as I had that theme, I could talk to the windows and the ceiling as well. They were all missing the mysterious lady who'd moved on. By the time Hank walked back into the room, the song was written. I sang it for him and asked what he thought. He thought I had a smash. I thought he was crazy. Turned out he wasn't.

SISTER

El Chico plays a big part in my story. It's a big chain of Mexican restaurants that was begun by Mama Cuellar and taken over by her five boys. It got so popular that John Wayne ate at the El Chico stand at the State Fair of Texas and Princess Grace had an El Chico–catered dinner at her palace to celebrate the Monaco centennial. I loved El Chico, not only for the food, but because they had hired me in their Fort Worth location to play dinner music on their brand-spanking-new Hammond B3 organ. That job helped me regain my health.

It wasn't as hectic or demanding as demonstrating the organ at county fairs or car shows. It was easier than dealing with the Hammond office, where the phones never stopped ringing. Quitting Hammond freed me up. Being a working mom with three young ones, I felt myself pulled in a half-dozen different directions. There were certain students I wanted to keep because teaching was my heart. I loved helping promising young musicians. But even easier than teaching, being an organist with a captive audience of happy diners munching their enchiladas was pure delight. I got to play anything I wanted. I remember "Stardust" was my first featured song. But there were dozens of others. I might play Ruby and the Romantics' "Our Day Will Come" or Johnny

Cash's "Ring of Fire." I had a wide repertoire, songs that seemed to please the patrons as much as they pleased me. I didn't have to sell a thing. I could actually relax. Relaxing was the blessing. Relaxing, especially by playing beautiful songs, was my way back to peace of mind. That peace of my mind, though, didn't last long. The reason had to do with romance.

I had fallen for a man who was not my husband.

BROTHER

Bobbie and Mama Nelson came to visit me, Martha, and the kids in Nashville. That was always a good feeling. I hated how the family had split off, but there wasn't nothing much I could do about it. I could give Bobbie a few comforting words and she could do the same for me. I knew about her troubles.

Anyone who'd endured what she'd endured was bound to have emotional ups and downs. I was just glad that her hospital stay was short. Also glad to hear about her good gig at El Chico. Thank God Sister was back playing music that made her happy. I said I wished I had a band of my own 'cause she'd be the first one I'd hire. But I wasn't even close to being in that position.

At the same time, my current position had improved. That's 'cause Faron Young, a popular country singer, had recorded "Hello, Walls." The damn thing sold two million copies. That was the first certified hit of my life. Faron believed in the song so much that not only did he record it, he loaned me $500 before it was released to help me get by. Many months later, when the tune had topped the charts, I got a royalty check for $3,000.

Nearly fainted.

Instead I ran down to Tootsies, where Faron was drinking.

I ran up to him and kissed him on the lips. "Buddy," I said, "here's your five hundred back. You're a helluva guy." But Faron wouldn't accept it. He heard I'd bought some calves. "Gimme a calf," he said. I didn't consider that fair. A calf was hardly worth $500. Weeks passed and I tried shoving the $500 in Faron's pocket again. "No cash," he said. "One of your calves gotta be at least five hundred pounds by now. Still waiting for that calf." Flash-forward another six, seven years. By then my song royalties were rolling in real good. Bought a two-thousand-pound prize Seminole bull, rented a truck, and had it sent to Faron with a note that said, "Here's your calf."

But back to then. "Hello, Walls" was the first hit. Then came "Crazy." "Crazy" got to Patsy Cline in an appropriately crazy way. Her husband/manager, Charlie Dick, heard my version and got so excited he took me over to the house, where he woke up Patsy at one A.M. I didn't see that as a good way to get a lady to hear a song. I was wrong. Patsy loved it and recorded it the very next week. Only mistake she made was trying to copy my oddball behind-the-beat style of singing. Her producer Owen Bradley told her to forget Willie Nelson style and sing it Patsy Cline style. She did, and "Crazy" went crazy. I'm still getting royalty checks.

Billy Walker had a hit with "Funny How Time Slips Away," and Ray Price, whose voice I'd loved for years, had a hit with "Night Life." That led to Ray inviting me into his band, the Cherokee Cowboys. He needed a bass player. Well, hell, I'd never played bass, but I'd also never say no to Ray. I halfway figured out the instrument in a hurry and found myself out on the road. That's about the time Bobbie saw that my marriage to Martha had run its course. Bobbie, being Bobbie, never said anything to me. She's too smart to ever intrude.

But I knew she knew. She and I have always been able to communicate without words.

Bobbie had seen that Martha and I had been fightin' for ten long years. Martha had enough of me. As it turned out, Bobbie was having marital problems of her own. I hated hearing that 'cause after all she'd gone through with Bud, I was hoping that Paul Tracy might be someone who could bring some stability to her life. He did, but the stability didn't last.

SISTER

No two ways about it, it was my fault. Or maybe I shouldn't use the word "fault." Maybe I'm being harsh on myself. Like one of my good friends says, maybe I need to show myself a little compassion. Maybe I can do that now, but at the time of the explosion, I was still using words like "blame," and I was sure enough putting the blame on me.

How could I do otherwise? I could have resisted, but I didn't. I could have turned a cold eye, but I didn't. The man's name was Jesus Martinez Oriana. He was a waiter at El Chico. Everyone called him Jesse. He was born in Mexico and spoke excellent English with a lilting Spanish accent. He had dark eyes and thick wavy hair. He displayed wonderful manners. He was kind, warm, and especially appreciative of my music. When I arrived every evening, he greeted me with a smile. He never failed to tell me how much my songs lifted his spirits. He knew I was married and kept his distance. At the same time, I felt his attraction to me and increasingly I felt mine to him. At evening's end, when the last diners had left, sometimes he'd approach me to ask me to play another song. He loved "Bésame Mucho," as did I. We both knew the theme of that song: the desire to be kissed. But for months that kiss never came. He was discreet, and so was I.

Yet I couldn't deny my feelings. My husband, Paul, had done nothing wrong, but I had little to say to him. We weren't on the same emotional level. He understood from the start that I didn't love him. He had to know because I never said the words. In contrast, he *always* said those words to me. Deep down, he knew I had married him only for the sake of security. But he got himself to believe otherwise. He went into denial. He convinced himself that I did, in fact, love him. He had no real reason to think that. I wasn't affectionate with him, and our sexual chemistry was always lackluster. In fact, we had stopped being sexual. As a sensual woman, and a romantic one as well, I was vulnerable. Looking back, I can see that I was looking for love, body and soul, the name of a song that I often played at El Chico as Jesse passed by carrying plates of fajitas and burritos. Jesse also used his own money to buy me sheet music written by Mexican composers, beautiful songs that I was pleased to learn and play. He had a beautiful voice and sometimes, after the place had emptied, he'd sing along.

During one evening after the restaurant had closed, I remained seated at the organ, playing love songs—"Sincerely," "Red Sails in the Sunset," "Misty"—that always warmed my heart.

Jesse came over and placed his hand on mine. That's all it took—that one simple act. I felt myself melting. I felt myself yearning. I felt myself moving in his direction. That was the night, in the apartment where he lived alone, that we did what we had both been dreaming of doing for so long.

There was another song that Doris Day had made popular called "Secret Love." I played it often. I identified with the sentiment, especially the idea that a secret love is impatient to be free. But I also knew that song's climax—the declaration that "my secret love is no secret anymore"—was something I could not realize. For the sake of my family, my children, and my marriage, my secret had to remain secret. So Jesse and I carried on secretly. After the death of Bud and in the aftermath of my breakdown, I felt restored. For the first time in years, I actually felt whole, nourished. It's one thing to be loved. It's another to give love. After Bud, Jesse was the first man to whom I could actually give love.

Remember, these were the sixties, when interracial couples, especially in Texas, were looked down upon and frequently harassed. In the eyes of many, a white woman with a Mexican man was no different than a white woman with a black man. Latinos have suffered cruel discrimination in Texas. When we went out on our secret rendezvous, people gave us dirty looks. Others actually said ugly things to our face. I was aware that our affair was doubly forbidden—first because I was married and second because he was of another ethnicity—but passion overwhelmed everything. Passion had brought me back to life again. Beyond the passion, there was a friendship I could count on, a man who understood all I'd gone through. I wish I could say that man was Paul, but it just wasn't. Jesse had the sensitivity that Paul lacked. I couldn't resist Jesse. I couldn't deny myself the satisfaction of being with someone who became my soulmate.

From time to time I'd call Willie because, of all the people in the world, I knew he'd understand. He'd gone through the same thing with Martha. She was the mother of their three children, but her fiery temperament had proved too much for Willie and Willie's wandering ways had proved too much for her. He too had found a soulmate, whose name was Shirley Collie.

BROTHER

I had a lot going on. I'd signed a solo deal with Liberty Records in L.A., but the album didn't go anywhere. I was making money as a writer, but as a singer my style didn't make much of a mark on the country charts. It would be years before I could say that I had something of a successful solo career.

Out on the road as one of Ray Price's Cherokee Cowboys, I'd met my friend Biff Collie, a deejay, and his wife, Shirley, an artist in her own right. Shirley was a fine singer whose specialty was yodeling, a technique requiring all sorts of control. Shirley also played bass and wrote first-rate songs. All-around great musician. We recorded a duet. Even though neither of us wrote the song—Hank Cochran did—the title just about summed up the sexual vibe we felt in the studio. The song was called "Willingly." To make a long story short, Shirley was willing and so was I. Fortunately, for reasons I never understood but always appreciated, Biff was understanding. Predictably, Martha wasn't. Martha was fit to be tied, but Martha was always fit to be tied. And had every right to be. Divorce was inevitable.

One of the reasons I was so taken by Shirley—in addition to her being a gorgeous redhead—was our harmony. The way I fool with the beat, I'm a tricky singer. Not everyone can or should follow me. But Shirley heard exactly what I was doing. Without even trying, she could blend her voice with mine. It was a natural thing. She could sing background, sing unison with me, and also provide just the right flair of pretty yodeling. Like me, she was country. She grew up in Chillicothe, Missouri, and her roots were the same music that nourished me. For a long while we nourished each other.

By 1963, the year I turned thirty, Shirley and I were married. I left Ray Price, and she and I formed a little trio with the great steel guitarist Jimmy Day, called the Offenders. Come to think of it, Offenders could be an earlier version of the Outlaw label used to describe me in the seventies. When it came to music, Shirley and I didn't care who we offended. We were set on playing the music we liked. Period. Might sound like offbeat western swing to some or too jazzy to others. Made no difference. We were into having fun. We played any dump that would have us, low-rent barrooms and seedy ballrooms all over Tennessee, Texas, Oklahoma, Louisiana, Arizona, and California. Pay us and we'd play. Shirley had her own spot on the show, I had mine, and then we'd croon together. It was a good music period for me. I was inspired to write songs like "Half a Man" and "Home Motel." "Half a Man" had a strange lyric. It was about how dismemberment might free a man from a lying woman. I located "Home Motel" on Lost Love Avenue, where a guy, crying the blues, lives a lonely life. Critics might speculate that the songs had something to do with my own life, except they didn't. They were just stories I invented. Personally, I was happy with Shirley.

Martha had the kids, she'd remarried, and, feeling the

need to connect with family, I moved back to Texas. Shirley didn't mind living in Fort Worth. She and Bobbie got along great. Everyone gets along great with Bobbie. But I knew Bobbie was having some problems. If I was nearby, maybe I could help.

SISTER

At the Hammond M3, 1965

No one could help because no one knew. Jesse was an El Chico employee. I was the organ player. We saw each other six evenings a week under the most proper circumstances. He was popular with his colleagues. I was popular with the diners. Sometimes if I played a Mexican song, Jesse would sing along. The customers loved that. Everything was going well. It was a respectable and appropriate relationship. Except it wasn't.

We found time to meet at his apartment, sometimes in the

afternoon before I began work at the restaurant, sometimes after closing hours. For me, it was about more than the warmth and romance of the connection. After my hysterectomy, it was also my way of feeling like a woman again. I couldn't give Jesse children, but I could give him my body and soul. I had tried but failed to give my heart to Paul. Paul was used to my silence, my inability to declare my love for him, but now Paul was sensing something else.

Just as a woman knows when her man is untrue, the same is true for many men. It was certainly true for Paul. When I came home late, he began questioning me closely. I lied about a private party in the restaurant where I was paid to play. Maybe he believed the lie, but he also couldn't help but see a glow surrounding me. Jesse was making me happy. Paul wasn't. Paul knew something was awry.

When he started showing up at El Chico at unexpected times, just to check in on me, I got concerned. I told Jesse we'd have to be extra careful. At first, I don't think Paul suspected Jesse. He just thought my lover was probably some customer who'd heard me play at the restaurant.

"I know you got someone," he kept saying. "If I catch you, I'll kill you both."

I got scared.

"We're gonna have to stop," I told Jesse.

Jesse was a reasonable man—a good man—and he readily agreed.

For several months we stopped seeing each other. Paul calmed down. He stopped screaming and throwing around accusations. It seemed like I could relax. I did, and that's when all hell broke out.

BROTHER

Shirley and I didn't stay in Fort Worth for long. I could have hung around, but Shirley wanted to get off the road. She saw Fort Worth as another stopgap half-home. A country girl, she wanted a permanent home with land around it. She was looking to move somewhere around Nashville.

It took a while to convince me 'cause in Fort Worth I'd taken up boxing. It helped my head. It was the first of a series of strenuous workout programs that would help me throughout my life. It wasn't helping that I was still drinking. It also wasn't helping that I was one of those stupid drunks who liked to take on the biggest bruiser in the bar. Some people drink and get mellow. Others drink and get manic. When I drank, I got dumb and violent. Fact is, I was too drunk to remember the times when tough guys kicked my ass for getting in their face. But I know it happened. My only salvation was reuniting with Fort Worth native son Paul English. He came back into my band as the drummer and, during my drinking binges, looked out after me. You could mess with me, but don't mess with Paul.

The pleasures of pot were a ways off. I'd tried smoking a joint years earlier. Nothing much happened. When I was on the road with Ray Price, I went to his hotel room one night and noticed a towel under his door.

"What is this stuff?" I asked Ray.

"Mexican dirt weed."

"Stinks to high heaven."

"Yeah, but it'll get you high as hell."

Took a toke, but nothing happened. What was working for Price still wasn't working for me. At the time, I was a Chesterfield smoker and too stupid to know what tobacco was doing to my lungs. Booze was also taking its toll on my brain. Not only did liquor turn me into an aggressive fool, it hung me over. And to get over the hangover required more drinking. The whole operation generated negative energy. Took me a long time to learn that lesson. Too damn long.

Same thing was true with pills. At that time, among country singers the go-to picker-uppers were bennies. Benzedrine was among the first amphetamines. That stuff cranked you up and had you going for days. Perfect for long-ass road trips, but like with booze, the comedown was decidedly unpleasant. The pillheads I knew were all jumping out of their skin. That nerve-racking feeling wasn't anything I wanted.

On the upside, Shirley's idea about locating some land and settling down turned out good. We found seventeen beautiful acres north of Goodlettsville, Tennessee, not far from the Kentucky border. Ridgetop, a farming community, was just what the doctor ordered. The farm on Greer Road was off the beaten track but close enough for me to get to Nashville in under an hour. The property included a sprawling ranch-style house set on a hill thick with cedar, pine, and weeping willow trees. The soil was rich red clay. Vegetable gardens, flower gardens, chicken coops, pigpens, horse corrals—I could finally see myself living the farmer's life, at least part of the time. Music would never go away, the road would never stop calling, but having a homestead large enough to house my entire family—Mom's and Dad's new families included—was a dream I could see coming true.

The big reason I could afford the Ridgetop farm wasn't my playing as much as my writing. I was lucky enough to keep having hits. One came as a complete surprise. I wrote "Pretty Paper" back in Fort Worth during Christmastime. Came about because I'd seen a man without legs selling wrapping paper in front of Leonard's department store. The way he called out the words, "Pretty paper, pretty paper for sale!" got to me. I made up a song about it—decades later I'd write a whole novel about it—and, as you might expect, called it "Pretty Paper."

Since I had a record deal, I thought I'd sing the song myself, but my friend Fred Foster sent it to Roy Orbison, who cut it first. That was fine with me. Roy was a big star, and I wasn't. When Roy's version hit big, I couldn't have been happier. I don't have to sing my own songs. Fact is, many of my songs sound better when other singers sing 'em. For instance, I sure as hell can't sing "Night Life" better than Aretha Franklin. Conversely, a little later in my career I also learned that sometimes when I sing other people's songs, they sell better than when I sing my own. I can't tell you why. The mystery of the record-buying public remains a mystery. Public taste defies predictions, defies critics, and defies artists desperately looking to please the public. Truth is, I like that unsolved mystery. Once you solve such mysteries, they're no longer mysteries and life is less fun.

Ridgetop was big fun. My dream of the whole Nelson family living in one spot came true. It took a while, and it didn't start out exactly smooth. Fact is, one of the first people to come up there from Texas was Bobbie, who arrived with Mama Nelson, Randy, Michael, and Freddy.

When I saw Sister come up the driveway and greet me at the front door, she was in tears. I wanted to know what was wrong. She said she was running for her life.

SISTER

I'm in trouble," I said to Willie on the phone.

"Then throw the boys in the car and get up here. Got lots of room for you, Mama Nelson, and the boys. You'll be safe here. Leave now."

I did. I left in a panic. Jesse and I had been careless. We thought that Paul was no longer suspicious and, though we stopped meeting in Jesse's apartment, I think Paul might have been spying on us at El Chico, walking by and looking through the window. He probably saw Jesse talking to me when he should have been waiting tables. Paul was getting crazier by the minute. After dinner he once even brandished his pistol and repeated the threat: He'd have no hesitation using it if one day he ever caught me with another man.

It blew up over a mere coincidence. I was walking alone through a shopping center when, by chance, I happened to see Jesse. We stopped to stay hello. We didn't hug, kiss, or even touch each other. But it turned out that Paul had followed me and saw what was, in fact, an innocent encounter. He knew Jesse as the waiter from El Chico, where I'd been working for months. He put two and two together. He didn't approach us at the shopping center, but when I got home his eyes were blazing red. He was out of his mind.

The boys were there along with Mama Nelson. But that

didn't stop Paul from taking out a pistol, putting it to my head, placing his finger on the trigger, and saying, "I'm going to blow your brains out." I was shaking, Mama Nelson was pleading with him, the boys were screaming. I think it was only the presence of my sons that saved me. As enraged as he was, he couldn't murder me in front of my children. Instead, he stormed out of the house.

Petrified, Mama Nelson and I packed up whatever we could, got the boys into the car, and drove seven hundred miles to Nashville. Never before had I been so glad to see my brother. He was so welcoming, so loving, so reassuring, so dedicated to my welfare that he said all of us should move in with him and stay permanently. I couldn't do that. He already had so much going on. His ex-wife, Martha, had remarried, left husband number two, and was turning the children—Lana, Susie, and Billy—back over to Willie. That meant Willie's new wife, Shirley, who had no kids of her own, suddenly had three. Willie was thrilled to have his children back, but I knew that would have a big impact on his marriage. I didn't want to burden him with more worries.

"No worries at all," he insisted. "You belong here."

Willie wanted to protect me, but I felt sure I could find my own way. Besides, something else was pulling at me: my love for Jesse.

Jesse had been given a promotion. El Chico was sending him to Austin, where they were opening a new restaurant with Jesse as the maître d'. He wanted me to relocate to Austin so that, free of Paul, we could finally be together. He also said that El Chico, realizing I had been good for business in Fort Worth, wanted me playing organ at their Austin restaurant. I could work there with Jesse as many nights a week as I liked. The offer was attractive, even irresistible. The only thing that held me back was something Jesse had told me a few months after we'd begun our relationship. He said he'd wanted to tell me the first night we were together but was afraid that the revelation would keep us apart. His fear was probably right. I might have backed off. But by the time I learned the truth it was too late. I was already in love. The truth added to my guilt, but it didn't end our love affair.

Jesse had a wife and children living in Mexico.

BROTHER

I don't want to sound too highfalutin, but I guess I'd have to call myself a poet. I say that because when I write about love I don't write realistically. I write poetically. That's another way of saying that I allow the mystery of love to say what it has to say. Even now I'd be hard-pressed to define love. I know God's love is pure. God's love is everywhere and in everything. But worldly love is flawed love and lots of times confused love. That's why I'm the last to judge anyone's love affairs. Around the time that Bobbie and I were going through tumultuous changes with our various spouses, I sat down and wrote a song called "I Never Cared for You." This was the midsixties, when I was living up on Greer Road in Ridgetop and watching Shirley trying to be a mom to my children.

The sun is filled with ice and gives no warmth at all
And the sky was never blue
The stars are raindrops searching for a place to fall
And I never cared for you
I know you won't believe these things I tell you
I know you won't believe
Your heart has been forewarned
All men will lie to you

And your mind cannot conceive
Now all depends on what I say to you
And on your doubting me
So I've prepared these statements far from true
Pay heed—and disbelieve

If you ask me to explain these lyrics, I'm gonna balk. I wasn't talking about the troubles Sister was going through. I wasn't even talking about my own troubles. And yet, reading the lines over today, it seems like I was saying that love has its dark side. That happiness today can be misery tomorrow. That vows made at midnight can die by morning.

I was also writing during a period when I was watching my own recording career go through a kind of death throes. My reputation as a writer had grown, and I had enough records out there to finally get a spot on the *Grand Ole Opry.* I'd be lying to say I wasn't thrilled—the *Opry* was the most popular show in the history of all country music—but I'd also be lying to say that the thrill lasted long. First obstacle was being told I couldn't use my own band. I was just part of the ensemble. Second obstacle was that my song selection was strictly restricted. Only the material the *Opry* operators felt worthwhile went on the show. For an oddball like me, that didn't work. Third obstacle was that, despite the exposure, the *Opry* cut down on my touring. I was contracted to do twenty-six *Opry* shows a year, meaning I couldn't be on the road as much as I wanted. Not only did I love the road, I needed the money the road provided. The *Opry* pay was paltry.

I quit after a season and switched over to Ernest Tubb, who had a TV show of his own. Since Tubb saw himself as the country Andy Williams, I had to follow suit. That meant going from sparkly cowboy getups to turtlenecks and khaki slacks. But Ernest's earnest attempt to sell me as a solo star didn't work. My next move was working at RCA with Chet Atkins, Nashville's producer king. Loved Chet and always will. Chet wanted me to sing hit songs by other country artists. Said that was the surest way to reach the masses. I didn't mind. I liked singing songs by George Jones and Harlan Howard. I grew up on Bob Wills's "San Antonio" and loved recording it. Chet had the good idea of using Ernest Tubb's band to back me up. The cover photo of the resulting record showed the cleanest-cut Willie you've ever seen. Looked like I just came from the barbershop. Only thing that bothered me was the title. Chet called it *Country Favorites—Willie Nelson Style.* Well, if we were going for the masses, didn't that mean reaching *beyond* the country market? Don't get me wrong. Country's my foundation, but I'm of the mind that music is music and that my music should reach everyone. When I brought this up to Chet, he was understanding but unyielding. He kept the title as is. He said, "One step at a time, Willie." Couldn't argue with that. Small steps are fine, but I was a lot more interested in giant leaps. Wasn't sure yet what those leaps would look like—that was in my future—but my spirit was restless.

The solo work I'd done in Nashville was fine. Every time I stepped into a studio, I learned something new. But there were always the restrictions of following the vision of a producer whose central concern was commerce. My central concern, then and now, was simply expressing my heart—and commerce be damned.

SISTER

It was a bold move, but I knew I had to make it. Leaving Ridgetop, I drove back to Fort Worth and put a plan in place: sneak back into the house in Fort Worth, grab whatever I could grab, and run down to Austin with my children in tow. My neighbors helped. I parked a few blocks away and called them to learn when Paul was out of the house. The minute he was gone, Mama Nelson, the boys, and I furiously filled a few suitcases. Mama Nelson decided to stay with Aunt Rosa. Her health had started to fail, and she wasn't able to relocate with us. Naturally that broke my heart. Mama Nelson was my rock. But I understood that the physical challenge was too much. If she could have come with us, she would have. She kept telling me I was strong enough to do this on my own. I wanted to believe her but was not sure I did.

Our departure, carried out in fear and desperation, was so hasty that I only took a few clothes for the boys and myself, cooking utensils, and a small portion of my sheet music catalog. I left behind my organ and instead took a spinet, a small and portable keyboard far more manageable than the massive Hammond.

We found a cramped little rental apartment in Austin. After a week or two, I drove back to Fort Worth with the boys to reclaim my organ. I needed it for my job at the El Chico where Jesse was working as the maître d'. I rented a U-Haul and when the neighbors said the coast was clear—Paul was gone for the day—my sons and I loaded up my instrument and drove back down to Austin.

Understandably, Randy, Michael, and Freddy weren't happy. Our house in Fort Worth was nice. This apartment was nasty. Of all people, the Fletchers were willing to help. They'd sold their farm in Vaughan and moved to Clifton, just north of Waco. They said they'd take the boys for the summer. I was a little skeptical, but I agreed. We'd gone from a pretty home in Fort Worth to a bare-bones rental in Austin. With my sons gone, I hoped to make enough money to improve our living condition by the time they returned in the fall.

That June the Fletchers invited me to see my children. All our reunions were wonderful except for this one. When I arrived, the person I saw was Paul Tracy.

"What are you doing here, Paul?" I asked.

"The Fletchers invited me," he said.

"Oh," was all I could reply.

I'm not sure why they did that. I want to give them the benefit of the doubt. Maybe they didn't know his violent history. Maybe they didn't realize the extent of his fury. Maybe they hadn't been told that we had to escape from him. Maybe they assumed that since he had been a surrogate dad to my boys for several years, he simply wanted to see them. Of course he could have done that when I wasn't there. But the Fletchers invited Paul to Clifton on the very weekend of my visit.

It turned into a horror movie. After our initial greeting, Paul got into my car before I had time to react. He was already out of his mind. He had a gun in one hand and a roll of tape in another. He said he was going to bind my mouth and shoot me in the head. Once again, it was my boys who saved me. When they heard me struggling to get out of the car, they started screaming, frantically banging on the windows and jumping on the hood. That brought Mr. Fletcher out of the house. Paul released me. He rode off. It took me all that day and the next to regain my sanity. Mr. Fletcher said he had no notion of Paul's history. I wanted to believe Mr. Fletcher. I also wanted to take my boys back with me to Austin at the end of August, but the Fletchers promised them motor scooters if they stayed in Clifton for the school year. Boys being boys, I couldn't blame them. But I also couldn't help but break down. I had lost my children for a second time, again to the Fletchers, though under very different circumstances.

Other than the El Chico gig, I had nothing. I was truly starting over. I loved Jesse but felt increasingly guilty. He belonged to his wife and children, not to me. He always sent them money. The only thing standing in the way of his reunited family was me. I felt—and Jesse agreed—that he should send for them. But because of the pleasure of our passionate encounters, he kept putting that off. We tried to stop seeing each other but couldn't. He was persistent. I was willing, I was weak, and I was racked with remorse. How would this thing ever stop?

At the same time, I needed to make money. El Chico hardly paid enough to cover my expenses. For a long while I struggled. I knew Willie would always loan me money, but being proud and knowing that I had earned my own living before, I was determined to earn my own living again. I approached other restaurants that might hire a piano player. None of them had any interest in me. For weeks, I kept offering my services, only to hear from a manager or owner that diners wanted to concentrate on conversation and food, not music.

The change came unexpectedly. One of the most historic buildings in the city was the Stephen F. Austin Hotel on 700 Congress Avenue in the heart of downtown. Built back in the twenties, the Austin is an architectural jewel. It housed Lyndon Johnson's first campaign headquarters when he ran for the House of Representatives in 1937. By the midsixties, though, the building had fallen into sad neglect. Then came its renaissance. It was refurbished and reopened just in time for a major change in Texas law that allowed liquor by the drink. Previously, cocktails could only be served in private clubs. Now you could sit in the Austin Hotel's elegant lobby and order anything you liked. The manager, who had heard me play at El Chico, asked whether I could play piano as well as organ. I assured him that I could. Piano was my first love.

"Great," he said. "I want you to play during cocktail hour. You'll add to the sophistication of the setting."

I was flattered and excited. He bought a beautiful Baldwin grand and hired me to play six nights a week. It was a dream job. Not that I don't love the Hammond, but nothing will ever replace a concert piano. The richness of its tone is incomparable.

The Stephen F. Austin Hotel sat only a few blocks from the state capitol, so it wasn't at all unusual to see well-known politicians making requests for songs. I'm proud to say that I could honor almost all those requests. Over the years, my knowledge of popular music kept growing. I'm blessed with a good memory of melodies. Other hotels, like the Chariot Inn, hired me to play on those evenings when I wasn't at the

Austin. Some restaurants, like the upscale Polonaise atop the Westgate Building, began using me during lunchtime as well as dinner.

Yet as my professional life stabilized, my personal life did not. Jesse and I were still a couple. Many times I cut off the relationship and many times I relented. The situation had to be resolved. But how? My current method of simply asking him to leave me alone wasn't working. He'd call, I'd say no, but then I'd cave in. Sometimes he'd go to Mexico to visit his wife and children. During one of those trips, my mother came to Austin, and the Fletchers drove the boys in to see their grandmother.

I was going to confide to Mom about Jesse, but I didn't. I was so glad to see her I didn't want to burden her with my problems. She was having too much fun enjoying her grandsons. Besides, we never had mother-and-daughter talks of that nature. The truth is that I never really discussed Jesse with anyone. Because he was around so often, Jesse got to know my boys. They liked him. I wish I could have introduced him to my extended family, but I didn't. Our affair remained secret.

SOMEONE SAID TO me that you're as sick as your secrets. That made sense to me. This secret love was slowly eroding my sense of self-worth. It just had to stop. That's when I took matters into my own hands. There was only one way to decisively and permanently cut it off with Jesse. My solution was to marry another man who had been pursuing me. I know it sounds crazy, and I'm sure it was, but it's what I knew I had to do to change a situation that I clearly couldn't change on my own. I needed to take a drastic step. There's something definitive and safe about the idea of marriage. Marriage means security. A new marriage would insulate me from the impossibility of my relationship with Jesse. I convinced myself that marriage would make things easier.

But, as you can guess, that only made things harder.

BROTHER

While I was still fooling around with the Nashville music machine, unsuccessfully trying to make it work for me, I met a couple of other characters who had similar challenges.

I'd run into Waylon Jennings when I was working in Phoenix. The whole town was talking about this fella playing JD's, a football-field-size club close to Arizona State. I went over to see what all the fuss was about. Turned out that Waylon was a fellow Texan from just outside Lubbock. He was rough and ready to bust through any and all musical barriers. He was country, but he was singing rock 'n' roll as well. Fact is, he'd been Buddy Holly's protégé. Buddy produced Waylon's first record and took him on tour as his sideman. Blind luck kept him off the plane that crashed, killing Buddy, the Big Bopper, and Ritchie Valens.

Me and Waylon became fast and forever friends. It was Waylon who first said that Nashville wasn't for me. He said Nashville was for conformists. Nashville would drain me dry. I'd never make it in Nashville. What made Waylon's warnings so funny was that he wound up in the very place he told me to avoid: Nashville. One day I was over at the RCA studios and looked up to see my good buddy Waylon. I wanted to know what in hell he was doing there. Well, sir, like me, he'd signed up with Chet Atkins. Like me, he was looking for that big crossover hit. Because folk music was popular, RCA was trying to sell him as country folk. Waylon and I were destined to learn the same lesson the hard way. It was hard because we were both country boys who, despite our natural inclination to buck the system, were overly impressed with the powers that be. Somewhere in our minds we thought those powers had the key to our success. They didn't. It would take us a few more years to find the courage to carve out our own trail.

Merle Haggard was another trailblazer I met in the sixties, another brother, another don't-try-to-box-me-in individualist. On the outside, Merle could be crusty and cranky, but on the inside he was sweet as sugar. His voice had a sugar-and-salt sound that made him one of the best singers in American music. He was also a helluva writer. Just as Buddy Holly mentored Waylon, Merle had a great mentor in Buck Owens. Merle had been in and out of trouble for much of his childhood, but once he was released from San Quentin and started writing and recording, there was no stopping him. "I'm a Lonesome Fugitive" put him on the map. There was a lot to Merle. He was a seeker. His songs reflected the depth of his spirit. Like me, he was a believer who wasn't afraid to challenge conventional theology. Also like me, he was a poker player. It was during those card games, which went on for some six decades, that we had our best metaphysical discussions. We were both Christians with our own take on religion.

"Reincarnation doesn't exactly fit in with my faith," Merle would say.

"Maybe your faith needs to be challenged," I'd respond.

"I challenge it every day. The thing is, we change but God doesn't. We need to accept God the way he is—not the way we want him to be."

"You got to accept the fact that my full house beats your three kings."

Merle would throw down his cards and say, "Using theology to distract an opponent ain't exactly Christian, Willie."

"Poker ain't a charitable institution."

"You show no mercy."

"What I'm showing is this full house."

UP ON MY Greer Road farm, I spent a little of my own money on pigs. I'd loved pigs ever since I was kid. Now, as an adult, I turned into a hog-raising fool. I say "fool" 'cause I really didn't know what I was doing. I built a pigpen with a fatal flaw: The hogs could slip under the bottom of the fence, meaning I was running every which way to try to catch those slippery critters. I also overfed the pigs to where several of 'em got sick. I loved farming but never really did find a way to turn that love into profit.

What I loved most was finally having enough land to house many members of my family. There were trailers and little houses scattered all around the property. My dad, Ira, and his wife, Lorraine, came to live at Ridgetop along with my stepbrothers, Doyle and Charles, who by then had families of their own. Even my former wife, Martha, who wanted to be close to our kids, found a place down the road and moved in with her new husband, Mickey Scott. Besides the family, all sorts of other folks—like my pal Paul English and his wife, Carlene, and my bass player Dan "Bee" Spears—were up there as well.

Because my song royalties were rolling in, I could lose money on pigs and still have enough to buy up more land overrun by chickens, ducks, and geese. My pride and joy were my horses. Bought me Tennessee Walkers, two palominos, two ponies for the kids, and my own quarter horse, the noble Preacher. Even learned how to calf rope.

Evenings were mighty pleasant because the boys from town liked coming to play poker or have a guitar pulling session 'round the fireplace. On any given night, I'd be shooting the bull with Roger Miller or Mel Tillis.

There were other kinds of shootings. When Ray Price asked me if I'd look over one of his prize roosters while he went on the road, I said sure. But when the rooster killed a couple of Shirley's beloved laying hens, Shirley flew into a fit. She grabbed a rifle and aimed at the rooster. Shirley wasn't the best shot in the world and, afraid she might wind up killing the wrong animal, I took the rifle and did the deed myself. When I told Ray the sad news, he didn't take it well. He called it his prize rooster. I called it a killing rooster. I said there ain't one fightin' rooster in all of Tennessee worth one good laying hen. He said he'd never sing my songs again. He stayed mad for years. But then came the night I was watching TV and up pops Ray Price singing "Night Life." Called him the next day to thank him. "Still haven't forgotten about my rooster," he said. "It's just that that damn song of yours is too good not to sing."

The Ridgetop farm was a beautiful and long interlude in my life. Not saying it was all sunshine and gravy. There were some notable disputes. No family is without craziness. But overall it was amazing how the craziness never got out of hand. Except one time. That was the time Shirley saw a bill from a Houston hospital. I tried to play it off as no big deal. I told her that I had to go to the hospital for something minor.

Shirley wasn't buying that for one simple reason: The bill said the charges were for the birth of a baby girl, Paula Carlene, born to a Mrs. Connie Nelson. Shirley wanted to know who in the hell was Connie Nelson. Couldn't lie. Was caught flat-footed. Had to get the words out of my mouth.

"Connie's my girlfriend and Paula's our daughter."

SISTER

It was 1967. I was thirty-six. Bud Smith was twenty-four. I met him at a convenience store where he was working behind the cash register. We started talking about music. He played guitar and sang and was pleased to know that I played piano. When I told him where, he showed up at one of the hotel lobbies to hear me. He acted impressed. He was a nice-looking guy with a pleasant personality. He was interested in me romantically. I didn't feel the romance, but I needed to find a way to once and for all break it off with Jesse. Bud Smith couldn't wait to get me in bed and figured the quickest way was to propose marriage. For me, marriage seemed a surefire way to make Jesse understand that this time I was serious. Jesse had to turn his complete attention to his wife and children. I married Bud Smith like I married Paul Tracy, out of practicality. Clearly I hadn't learned much.

A few months later, Jesse died of a heart attack. The news shocked and saddened me beyond words. I don't want to believe that my rejection of him caused his death. But I also know that a broken heart is more than a phrase. It's a reality. I did break the man's heart. My heart was broken as well—by the impossibility of our love and the tragedy of his death.

By then, my boys were back in Austin. They were happy to be reunited with their mother. They sensed that my having a new husband might stabilize things. Bud Smith was a good guy. He was closer in age to my sons, then teenagers, than any other man I'd been with. Randy was seventeen, Michael fifteen, and Freddy fourteen. Bud treated them well. Bud was also happy—too happy as it turned out—to accompany me to my gigs. He began playing guitar and singing. Bud was not a great musician or singer. But he was my husband, and, especially at the start of our new marriage, I didn't want to criticize him or make him feel unworthy. It was an uncomfortable situation.

Sometimes a physical move can distract you from an emotional issue. I met an agent who said, "Bobbie, I can book you outside Austin and get you more money."

"More money than the Forty Acres Club?" That was my current gig, a prestigious venue across from the University of Texas.

"Yes, ma'am. I can book you at the Randolph Air Force Base in Universal City just outside San Antone. You interested?"

I was. Naturally my husband, Bud, came along and played, still unaware how he was hurting rather than helping my musical presentation. I just didn't have the heart to tell him the truth. The boys, now used to sudden changes and unexpected moves, came with me and enrolled in local schools.

I traded in my own Mustang for a 1967 Pontiac Firebird, a car that Randy loved. I needed that car to make the trek from San Antonio to Galveston, where I was also playing at the Balinese, a private club. Most times Bud looked after the boys. But then Randy, my oldest, came down with hepatitis. He got so sick I had to take him with me to Galveston, where he wound up in the hospital. That's when I started to feel overwhelmed again. I knew I needed a lot more help than my new husband could provide. I called Willie and told him what I was going through. Willie said what he'd been saying to me for years. "Come to Ridgetop and bring the boys. You're better off living up here with family."

I knew he was right. There was nothing to leave behind in San Antone and Galveston. So I made the move to Tennessee, and that became the start of a whole new chapter.

PART V

THE FAMILY STORY IN TENNESSEE...

BROTHER

This was what I'd always wanted—everyone coming together. Maybe because our mom had visited Bobbie in Austin, she realized how much she missed everyone. Around the same time that Bobbie, her boys, and her new husband, Bud, showed up on Greer Road, Mom and her husband, Ken "Kilowatt" Harvey, left their home in the Northwest and moved to Ridgetop. Although Mom and Dad were on opposite ends of the land, my parents were back with me and Bobbie for the first time since our early childhood. The circle was unbroken.

Goes without saying that Shirley had had enough of me. Few wives could put up with a man who has not only fallen in love with another woman but fathered a child with her as well. That beautiful child, Paula Carlene, was born October 27, 1969. Not long after, Shirley moved out. I hated hurting her, just as I hated hurting anyone I loved. Cheating on a woman doesn't mean you don't love her. Shirley was a great gal with a great talent. It would take time, but eventually we'd mend our ways and get to be friends again. By then I had married Paula's mom, Connie Koepke, a gorgeous young woman in her early twenties. Truth is, Connie had been my girlfriend for several years before becoming pregnant. By the beginning of 1970, she was living in Ridgetop with baby Paula. Connie got close to my kids with Martha—Lana, Susie, and Billy—and especially close to Bobbie. That didn't surprise me. Everyone likes confiding in Bobbie.

SISTER

Being back in the bosom of the family was beautiful. It was also healing. Randy's health improved, and of course my boys were thrilled to be with their cousins as well as both their grandparents. From time to time, Mama Nelson would come up from Fort Worth to visit. Willie's wife, Connie, was a doll. We became instant sisters, and I adored little Paula. Because Willie's farm was so big, we each had our separate places—whether a house or a trailer—that gave us enough room to breathe. Old anger could be forgotten. It was finally, as Willie has always wanted, family first.

Of course, things got a little dysfunctional. I'm thinking about the incident Brother calls the Great Shootout when, fortunately, none of the shots landed and no injuries were sustained, except those to our family pride. This was the start of the seventies. Willie's daughter Lana was married to Steve, a man prone to violence. When Willie learned he'd been violent with Lana, Willie got violent himself. He knocked Steve down. Steve managed to escape, but as he drove off, Willie took out his shotgun and blew out one of the tires on Steve's pickup. Later that day Willie was out in the pasture feeding his horses when Steve came roaring by and fired a shot that, thank God, missed Willie's head. Never a dull moment up on Greer Road.

Willie divided his time between the farm, recording in Nashville, and the road. My brother was close to all my boys—he treated them like sons—and knowing that Randy was eager to do some traveling, Brother had him driving the band trailer all around the country. Randy loved being with his uncle, but back in Texas, while still in school, he had fallen for Phyllis, the love of his life and the young woman he'd eventually marry. After several months in Ridgetop, Randy came to me. He knew how much it meant for the family to finally be reunited, but he was missing Phyllis something fierce. Would I be terribly hurt if he went back to Austin to be with his girl? I knew Phyllis was a wonderful person and gave Randy my blessing. Randy returned there and, as fate would have it, Austin would become the crossroads in the life of the Nelson family.

BROTHER

Bob Dylan surprised a lot of folks by recording in Nashville. Back in '66 he'd cut some of his *Blonde on Blonde* album there and in '69 his *Nashville Skyline* featured "Girl from the North Country," Bob's duet with Johnny Cash. My buddy Kris Kristofferson, a young genius songwriter himself, talked about how Dylan had opened the floodgates by extending the range of songwriting. We could write about whatever we wanted. I'd been doing that ever since I was a kid, but Bob definitely legitimized radical political subject matter. In the sixties, when the country was going crazy, that was a positive step. I also respected how Dylan respected country music.

What I didn't respect, though, was how the country music establishment was always looking to follow trends. I remember Waylon complaining about how the label insisted that he cut "Norwegian Wood," the song best sung by the Beatles. He was convinced the Nashville music execs were clueless. I had to agree. I did agree to sing songs like Joni Mitchell's "Both Sides Now" and James Taylor's "Fire and Rain." Sang 'em, though, not because I was chasing some fashion but because I liked the songs. Also sang Kris's "Sunday Mornin' Coming Down" and Merle Haggard's "Today I Started Loving You Again." I was convinced they were two of the best tunes out there. When it comes to music, I like to think I'm someone without prejudice. A song can be seventy years old or written last night. The writer can be a young woman or an old man. The critics can call the genre jazz or pop or country or folk. I don't care. If I like it, I'll sing it. I hope the composer is happy with my interpretation. But if she or he isn't, that's okay too. My aim is simply to be true to how I hear the song. For me to be satisfied, it has to be filtered through my own soul.

Meanwhile, I was still writing my own stuff. I'll always be writing. At the same time, I had a backlog of my own songs that I'd revisit when the mood struck me. When I wrote "Bloody Mary Morning," for instance, I had split my life in halves—half with Connie in Texas and the other half with Shirley in Ridgetop. I wrote the line "Temptation and deceit are still the order of the day." I was still drinking and not ready to stop. Bloody Marys were doing me no good. Chain-smoking Chesterfields was doing me even worse. Together, the booze and the cigarettes had me in a fog. And yet the song, even if it does sound like the confession of a man in full confusion, ain't half-bad. Sixty years later, I'm still singing it.

I've never seen songwriting as anything more than a way of taking whatever's going through my mind and putting it down on paper. I never try to be profound. Never try to preach or teach. Never try to figure out why I've written what I've written. It's just there. Thoughts turn to words, and words find a melody that helps 'em go down easy. If a song comes out silly, I leave it that way. If a song comes out romantic, well, that's sweet. If a song comes out on a record that no one remembers, that's fine. Or if a song somehow registers with folks and helps 'em get through their day, why, that's even better. Writing songs has helped me get through life. Sometimes I think writing songs—and playing them for people generous enough to pay their hard-earned cash to hear me sing 'em—is all that's kept me from going off the deep end.

Even while my solo career as an RCA recording artist continued to go nowhere fast—turning out album after album that never garnered big sales—I was going back to the clubs from Texas to California that kept me in business. Also kept me happy. It was great having my nephew Randy along for the ride. What I really wanted, though, was to have Bobbie join the band. It'd been way, way too long since we'd played together. Truth is, I never had a permanent piano player since I'd been with Bobbie in Bud Fletcher and the Texans. Never even tried looking for one. Bobbie couldn't be replaced. She also couldn't be convinced to go on the road 'cause Michael and Freddy were in school in Tennessee and Bobbie being Bobbie always needed to be close to her boys.

SISTER

When we first got to Willie's farm in Ridgetop, we stayed in a trailer. But soon I was earning enough money for us to rent a house in Greenbrier, just down the highway. My good fortune came from a fine restaurant outside Nashville called Dutchman's. They had me playing dinner music six nights a week. I loved interpreting divine songs like "Lara's Theme," the love theme from the movie *Doctor Zhivago*, and "I Left My Heart in San Francisco." What I loved even more was that my Freddy, even as a teenager, was good enough to work with me as a drummer. Nothing pleased me more than witnessing the blossoming of his talent.

Michael had another kind of talent. He was a brilliant student. When Willie was selling encyclopedias, he gave us a set. Michael read his way through all eighteen volumes. From a young age he had expressed his determination to go to college and eventually study law. I promised to support him in that effort. He kept up his straight-A grades. Of all the Nelsons, he was by far the most bookish. He thought clearly and wrote beautifully. I realized his gift for scholarship, and when he graduated from high school with high honors I beamed with pride.

Bud Smith and I were still a married couple. He was working at a nearby Burger King and probably felt a little overwhelmed by all the Nelsons surrounding him. He did the best he could to adjust. Just as I never felt romantically inclined toward Paul Tracy, I just didn't have romantic feelings for Bud. It wasn't his age. Older women and younger men—and vice versa—often hit it off. The age difference can make it even more exciting. It's just that Bud and I never really clicked. I wish it weren't so. I wish I could have used him at the Dutchman's gig, but he didn't fit in. He still hadn't developed his guitar playing or singing to a professional level.

In telling him that, I tried to be gentle. Everyone is sensitive. Everyone requires respect. And so I simply politely suggested that he practice more. He couldn't help but see that, although I didn't ignore him, my attention was on my boys, my brother, and especially my mom and dad. Having them around was such a treat. I always sought their company. People asked whether I felt resentment that they had abandoned us as children. I can honestly say no. Maybe those feelings existed when I was a kid. But as an adult who had gone through turbulent times myself, I understood how their own turbulent times had forced them to go their separate ways.

Ridgetop represented a reconciliation that only a man like Willie could have realized. The farming, the family, the glorious sunsets, the sense of well-being quieted my nerves and afforded me peace. But then, just when life was moving along at a pleasant pace, came an explosion no one saw coming.

BROTHER

I'm no good with dates, but December 23, 1970, is one I'm never gonna forget. Evening started out fine. I was at the King of the Road club in Nashville, named after my buddy Roger Miller's famous song. Roger was there that night, cracking us up with his endless supply of jokes, some clean, most of 'em not so clean. It was the annual Christmas party put on by club owner Lucky Moeller. I had thrown back more than a few when Lucky said I was wanted on the phone. It was Bobbie's son, my nephew Randy. He was so worked up I could hardly hear what he was saying. Didn't help that the rowdy party crowd was yelping it up. I tried to get everyone to quiet down so I could make out Randy's words. But no one paid me no mind. The crowd got even louder. "You're gonna have to scream, Randy," I said, "'cause the noise in here is getting worse by the minute." Randy did scream. He screamed at the top of his lungs. His words went through me like a knife.

"Uncle Willie," he yelled, *"your house is on fire! The whole thing's going up in flames!"*

First thing I asked was whether anyone was inside. No one. Everyone—Connie and the kids—was safe. Next thing I asked was whether the garage had also caught fire. Randy said no, but the flames were close. Thinking fast, I told Randy to hurry up and put my old beat-up car in the garage. Since insurance was going to cover the fire, why not get a new car out of the deal?

Raced home fast as I could. Got there after the fire trucks. They were hosing down the house, but the flames kept getting bigger. I went over to comfort my family. They were all huddled around, watching. A few were crying. I said not to worry. Long as no one was injured, we were okay. Before the whole thing collapsed, I decided there were a couple of things I needed to run in and rescue—my guitar Trigger (named, of course, after Roy Rogers's trusty horse) and a bag of primo Colombian pot. I'd just started smoking weed on a regular basis and wasn't about to lose a couple of pounds of good grass.

The calamity was caused by faulty wiring in the basement. The conflagration was something to behold. The fire blew my mind. But having your mind blown isn't always a bad thing. Sometimes disruption and even material destruction can help you rethink your priorities. Sometimes your life needs to be blown up so you can start a new one. Something about that Ridgetop fire told me it was time to get a move on.

So I did.

SISTER

Brother moves by instincts. He's a deep thinker, but I've never known him to overanalyze. He lets his feelings direct him. After the house burned down, he took it as a sign to leave Tennessee and move his whole operation back to Texas. When he told me that, it felt right. He had a friend named Crash Stewart, a promoter who'd been booking Willie for years, who found a run-down dude ranch fifty miles from San Antonio in Bandera. There was a house for Willie, Connie, and the kids, and cabins for everyone else. It was a place where Willie's traveling tribe could settle down for the winter.

Much as I wanted to, I couldn't join them. I decided to stay behind in Greenbrier principally because Michael was in his last year of high school and doing very well, and I wanted to personally enroll him in Austin Peay State University in nearby Clarksville. I also thought it'd be a good idea to hold on to my job at Dutchman's, where I'd built up a good following and was able to save up a little money. Freddy decided to go to Bandera with his uncle Willie, and Randy was already back in Texas with Phyllis. Randy took up law enforcement and was training to be a deputy sheriff in Rollingwood, just outside Austin.

I was proud of all my boys. They hadn't had an easy time

of it, yet they proved resilient. They grew into strong young men. It was a thrill to drive Michael to Austin Peay and settle him into his dorm. College would prove a snap for Michael, who never lost sight of his ultimate goal—to attend law school and become a practicing attorney.

My marriage barely survived these years in Tennessee. I give Bud credit for hanging in. I tried, but I'm afraid I didn't give him much affection. During Michael's first semester at the university, he let me know he was okay on his own. That's when I decided to go back to Texas. With Willie gone, there was no reason to stay around. Austin sounded good to me. Randy and Phyllis were there. I knew I'd have no trouble finding work. The nature of that work, though, underwent a radical change.

BROTHER

Bandera had its own kind of beauty. There were hills and creeks and rivulets and, best of all, a golf course that called to me. Took to golf like a bee to honey. Golf became part of my life from then on. Something about smacking, chipping, and putting that little white ball fascinated me. Coming home to Texas also coincided with my conversion from booze and cigarettes to pot. This changed my life.

I believe it saved my life.

Took me way too long to admit that tobacco and liquor contained toxins that were injuring me. It should have been obvious, but when you're drunk or chain-smoking those cancer sticks, you ain't thinking straight. Whiskey and Chesterfields were flat doing me in. Increasingly, I saw how pot was mellowing me out. Liquor sped me up and made me aggressive. Pot slowed me down and made me reflective. What could be better? My switchover to weed coincided with some other changes happening in Bandera.

I started reading authors—like Edgar Cayce and Kahlil Gibran—who were pointing me to more expansive ways of thinking. Gibran talked about "spaces in your togetherness," explaining how love shouldn't be a chain. "Love one another," he wrote, "but make not a bond of love . . . even as the strings of a lute are alone though they quiver with the same music." Cayce has this thing about power of the mind. Father A. A. Taliaferro, an Episcopal priest in Dallas, mirrored Norman Vincent Peale, who had helped kick things off with his *Power of Positive Thinking* back in the early fifties. Another book of his was *You Can If You Think You Can.* The notion of eliminating negativity was a big deal, a major revelation. Of course I didn't pull it off entirely—who ever does?—but it was really important to have it as a goal.

All this influenced my songwriting. If you were an artist, you had to be living under a rock not to hear the way popular music was changing. The Beatles' *Sgt. Pepper's Lonely Hearts Club Band* had everyone talking about concept albums. Don't just string together a bunch of singles, but make a big statement, write a big story, paint some kind of musical landscape. I liked that challenge. Got my creative juices flowing. Also got me thinking back to some of the music I first heard when I was a kid. That was the gospel music played and sung by Mama and Daddy Nelson. That music never left my soul.

That music definitely was on my mind and in my heart when I turned out my first concept album, *Yesterday's Wine.* It was a record that had me, at age thirty-eight, in the most introspective mood of my professional life. Hanging out in Bandera, hitting the ball around this mangy golf course, wandering through the countryside at night under the light of the moon, I got to thinking. Why am I here? What is my purpose? What am I—and for that matter, all of mankind—trying to achieve?

Those questions formed the basis of my exploration. It felt good to leave the tried-and-true formula of songwriting and venture into places unknown. Maybe it was the comfort of being home in Texas. Maybe it was just being fed up with churning out Nashville-sounding albums year after year. I needed to challenge myself. Needed to get off cruise control and let the spirit lead me wherever it wanted to go.

I started writing about Perfect Man, the term I gave to Jesus, the gentle and compassionate Jesus that I'd seen in the eyes of my grandparents. As imperfect man, I looked to Jesus as the teacher of how divine and human love can be brought together. I wasn't preaching, I was reaching to write in a spiritual mode. One of the songs was called "In God's Eyes," where I see people as lambs gone astray and looking to be led home. I recorded the song I'd written a lifetime earlier, "Family Bible," which fit into this same mode of renewing my faith. Another key song was "It's Not for Me to Understand," a story about how we might not fully comprehend God's will, but it's our job to quietly allow that will to direct us. The songs were so heavy that, to lighten the mood just a little, I wrote "Me and Paul" about the crazy adventures my best buddy, drummer Paul English, and I had experienced over the years. I finished off the album with "Goin' Home," an out-of-body vision where I'm observing my own funeral. Not that I expected to die anytime soon. I just thought that would be another interesting way to keep up the dialogue with God.

RCA didn't think any of it was interesting. They didn't like the record. One exec called it my worst. Another said I was influenced by all this hippie stuff and asked whether I'd been smoking dope. The answer was yes and yes. I had been smoking dope. I liked the hippie attitude that stressed love over hate and peace over war. Young people and their music had certainly impacted me. At the same time, *Yesterday's Wine* did not impact the music industry. Sales were weak. My stock at RCA went down several notches. Some reviewers liked it, some didn't, but none of that mattered to me. I felt like I'd broken through a barrier. As a writer, being excited about my writing—and wanting to write more—is all that counts. Texas had me excited. That excitement climbed to a fever pitch in March of 1972 at the Dripping Springs reunion, a weekend music festival outside Austin. Austin turned out to be the key to the next big phase of my life.

SISTER

Entertaining at a party for Michael, the seventies

Austin was a godsend for all of us.

I worked at several dinner clubs in Lakeway, a resort area in the hill country just outside the city. Being surrounded by natural beauty was heaven. So was playing piano in a restaurant that overlooked Lake Travis. My son Randy found me a nice little house in Austin. After leaving Bandera, Freddy came to live with me and graduated from high school. By then, Bud Smith and I had split up. I was sorry that relationship didn't work out. But Bud didn't seem all that crest-fallen because he quickly found someone else—and I was happy for him.

The lawyer who handled the divorce was also a good friend, Joel Mitchell. Joel was one of the gentlemen who liked to congregate around the piano when I played the Austin supper clubs. He also helped Randy with several real estate transactions. The truth is that we became more than friends. We became intimate. Intimacy, though, didn't turn into long-term romance. Our friendship endured and brought me great comfort at critical times in my life. I treasured Joel not only for his brilliant mind and endearing personality, but also for his undying loyalty.

Returning to Austin, I found happiness as a single woman. My sons were prospering. Randy had his deputy sheriff job, Freddy had turned into a first-rate musician, and Michael was acing his way through college and eventually would enroll in law school at Memphis State. Good fortune smiled down on all of us. I found another steady job, this one at the Howard Johnson's on Interstate 35. Back then the HoJo restaurants were at their peak.

My goal was simple: stay close to my boys, work the supper clubs, and keep making a decent living. Meanwhile, Mama Nelson had started experiencing serious health problems. Willie and I moved her to a nursing home in Fort Worth. We visited her often and, though her body was weak, her spirit stayed strong.

After one of those visits, Willie made a casual remark that, at face value, didn't seem like a big deal. Yet it turned out to be the biggest deal of all. "Bobbie," he said, "you know we really haven't played together since 1951 when Bud Fletcher and the Texans broke up. That's twenty-one years. Don't you think twenty-one years is long enough?"

"I do."

"Well, then," said Brother, "we got to figure out a way to do something about that. We need a plan."

BROTHER

I think there's a divine plan. Like my song said, I don't have to understand the plan to see that it's being put in place by someone who sure ain't me. For example, I didn't tell Bobbie to move back to Austin. That was something she did on her own. I was happy being tucked away in Bandera. But once Bobbie settled in Austin, she kept saying how things were changing. She kept describing Austin as something altogether different from anywhere in Texas.

After Dripping Springs, I saw how Austin was a haven for the hippies, and how the hippies were open-minded 'bout all sorts of music. Also saw that Austin had its own version of San Francisco's Fillmore West called the Armadillo World Headquarters. It was one of those giant venues where folks came out to see Frank Zappa on a Friday and Ravi Shankar on a Saturday. When I booked in the 'Dillo I wondered how my band would be received. Didn't have to wonder long. Austin welcomed us with open arms. Austin was also home to Darrell Royal, the University of Texas football coach and one of my closest buddies, who loved music as much as sports. Like Bobbie, Darrell was always telling me I'd be happy in Austin.

Austin's progressive politics also made me comfortable. The antiwar position I'd taken for years didn't sit well in the rest of the Texas, but I didn't care. I followed my conscience. I found a like-minded constituency of fellow protesters. Both in '72 and '74, I played benefits for gubernatorial candidate Sissy Farenthold, and though she didn't win, I saw Austin as a city of winners. Musical winners. Spiritual winners. A place where hippies and hillbillies looked beyond labels and came together to hear good music. Once in a while a wise guy, seeing how I'd started braiding my long hair, said he absolutely had to know whether I was a hippie or a hillbilly. I passed him the joint and said, "Have a hit and decide for yourself."

SISTER

By the end of 1972, Willie had moved to Austin. He was living on Riverside Drive near Town Lake. His wife, Connie, was pregnant with their second daughter, Amy. Seemed like overnight Brother had become an Austin hero. He was the right man in the right place at the right time. Willie became everything to everyone. That brought me great pride. At the same time, I stayed on an independent course, working supper clubs and enjoying being close to Randy and Freddy. Michael was doing great at law school, and the four of us would always spend the holidays together.

On the visit to Mama Nelson in Fort Worth when Willie mentioned this plan for us to finally start making music together, he talked about Jerry Wexler, an owner and producer at Atlantic Records famous for his work with Ray Charles and Aretha Franklin. Even though Wexler's specialty was rhythm and blues, he loved Brother's music and was convinced that the Nashville music establishment hadn't done right by him. He offered a deal that was different from any deal that had ever come Willie's way. Wexler wanted Willie to be his own producer, pick his own material, and play with whichever musicians he wanted.

One of the reasons I'd never recorded with Willie before had to do with Nashville's proclivity to use a stable of studio musicians the producers felt were the best around. Willie never had any argument with the musicianship on the Nashville recording scene. But because his music is so peculiar to his own sensibility, Willie knows best who fits in most naturally with whatever he's creating. Jerry Wexler was the first one to understand. He set Willie free.

BROTHER

As phone calls go, this one turned out to be monumental. It began simply enough.

"You know my favorite Willie Nelson album?" asked Jerry Wexler.

"I have no idea."

"*Yesterday's Wine.*"

"That's not everyone's favorite."

"I love it, Willie, because it's you being you."

"Thanks, Jerry."

"I'm not looking for thanks. I'm looking for you to do more of the same."

"What do you mean?"

"I want you to do whatever you want. Get in the studio and follow your muse. Let it take you wherever it takes you."

Well, I'd been waiting fifteen years to hear words like that from a producer. Jerry also had other words.

"Cut the record in New York," he suggested.

"New York's a little too hustle-bustle for me."

"New York might help get the sparks flying. You've never recorded here before, have you?"

"Nope."

"Another reason to give it a try. New studio. New canvas."

"You gonna provide the studio musicians, Jerry?" I asked.

"Hell, no. You'll choose whoever you want."

I immediately thought of Bobbie. She was the main spark I'd been missing. I also thought of a gospel record. I was convinced a concept like that, so obviously uncommercial, would turn Wexler off. But it actually turned him on.

"I love gospel," he said. "I just recorded Aretha singing 'Amazing Grace' in a Los Angeles church. Let's go with gospel."

All this good man wanted was for me to be me. There was no way to get around it. He made it impossible for me not to go to New York. To get ready, the first call I made was to Bobbie. When it came to playing with Sister, Wexler had given me the plan I'd been praying for.

SISTER

Willie was excited. Willie's always excited about music, but this was a different kind of excitement. This was a way for us to go all the way back to our deepest roots.

"You pick the songs," he said. "You know them better than me. You'll know which ones will work best on a record."

I said, "Willie, you've been recording your whole life. I've never recorded before. I've never even been in a recording studio. I won't know what to do."

"Sure you will. You'll show me what to do. You've always shown me what to do. Recording in a studio is no big deal. You'll do great."

"I've never been to New York. I've never even been on a plane."

"Ever more reason to sign on. Flying is fun, and you'll get to see the Empire State Building."

I laughed and promised to get to work. That meant picking out songs. I knew the ones Willie wanted were those we'd sung as kids while Daddy Nelson was still alive. That meant music from our original hymnal at the Abbott United Methodist Church—"Precious Memories," "Will the Circle Be Unbroken," "Uncloudy Day," "Sweet Bye and Bye," "When the Roll Is Called Up Yonder," and "In the Garden." Before we got to New York, I worked out the arrangements, using Willie's bass player Bee Spears, steel guitarist Jimmy Day, electric guitarist Doug Sahm, and of course Paul English on drums. I kept it simple 'cause that's how Brother likes it. He added on a song called "The Troublemaker" that turned into the album title. Typical of Willie. He likes to see himself as a troublemaker, although in this case the troublemaker is Jesus, who is compared to the hippies, a benevolent soul going around calling for love and peace.

Doing those sessions with Willie, joy filled my heart. We were back in our childhood at the same time we were together in our adulthood. Our music merged like it always had. Time melted. Melodies flowed. Harmonies came naturally. Willie sang beautifully. Jerry Wexler was thrilled. He didn't have a single criticism. Matter of fact, all he said was, "Give me more." That's when Willie got an idea. Willie always has ideas.

BROTHER

The Shotgun Willie *session, New York City, 1973*

For good reason, Wexler was always pushing me. He liked the gospel record but now he wanted more. Now he wanted me writing. He said, "Willie, you sing great, you play guitar great, but no one writes better. While you're up here in New York, take off a few days, write a few songs, and record them with Bobbie and the boys. I'll give you all the studio time you need."

Turning down Jerry was tough 'cause I'd learned to love him. The man had great spirit. I told him I'd give it a try.

Wasn't easy. Hanging out in my hotel room reminded me of when I was in that little office in Goodlettsville, Tennessee, the day I wrote "Hello, Walls." No ideas were coming my way. So instead I wrote some nonsense lyrics about Shotgun Willie sitting around in his underwear, biting on a bullet, pulling out his hair, with his family there. Guess I was thinking about the time back in Ridgetop when I took a shot at my daughter's husband. My thoughts got even stronger. I started writing 'bout how you can't make a record if you ain't got nothing to say and you can't play music when you don't know nothing to play. Turned out to be a song about not being able to write a song. Called it "Shotgun Willie." That became the album title. Wrote a few more originals and also recorded with a harmonica player introduced to me by Coach Darrell Royal, Mickey Raphael, who was so good he's with me to this day. Mickey's one of the world's most soulful musicians on any instrument.

Did something else on *Shotgun Willie* in addition to singing some old Bob Wills songs. Sang Leon Russell's "A Song for You." Leon had become a big character in my life. He was the best showman I'd ever met. Besides being a raw soul singer and killer piano player, he addressed the younger generation of the late sixties and early seventies straight-on. He was one of them. At the same time, he was an old soul who loved country music to where he even adopted a country alter-ego identity—Hank Wilson. He also wrote standards, and I wondered if Wexler would object to me singing Leon's "A Song for You."

True to form, Jerry encouraged me to do it. While Nashville saw my phrasing as offbeat, Jerry saw it as being right on. He compared me to Sinatra, who was, in fact, the singer who taught me that you can play with the beat. You can adjust your phrasing any way that suits your style. You can bring the song to you rather than strain to make it sound "correct." The idea is to make it sound natural, conversational, completely personal. Later in life when I met Sinatra, first thing I said was that he was my favorite singer. His reply knocked me for a loop. He said I was *his* favorite singer. Hot damn!

The Atlantic Records experience put me on a new course. Most important, it brought me back together with Bobbie. When the sessions in New York were over I made it plain.

"Sister," I said, "you're now a member of the band."

SISTER

Playing piano on the Troublemaker *gospel album, New York City, 1973*

The band became a family. Willie gave the band that actual name—Family. By letting Willie play whatever he wanted with whomever he wanted, Jerry Wexler understood that family, and not for-hire studio musicians, was the key to Brother's musical happiness. It became the key to my happiness as well. I just hadn't realized how much I missed playing music with Willie. Much as I loved playing "Dancing in the Dark" or "Tenderly" at fancy supper clubs, that couldn't match the excitement of being part of Willie's band. Decades earlier, when we became professionals in Bud Fletcher and the Texans, Bud was just a figurehead, not an accomplished musician. Willie Nelson and Family was headed by a real mu-

sician who, after decades on the road and dozens of record-
ings, had finally come into his own.

Yet if I was to join the band, changes needed to be made.
Bee Spears was the first to explain. Bee, who came from San
Antone, had been Willie's bassist since the sixties. He was a
beautiful character and was part of Brother's inner circle. Bee
knew the scene inside out and was the only one to say that I
didn't look the part. I needed to change my style. For the venues I was used to playing, I wore evening dresses. Evening
dresses would hardly be appropriate for Family. Bee, who
called me Jobbie, said, "Look here, girl, you're gonna have to
leave your stove and your kitchen and get on the bus with us.
You're gonna have to get out of those cocktail-type costumes,
Jobbie, and get into some tight jeans and cowgirl boots."

Willie put it another way. "The dress code," he said, "is no
code." When someone brought up the long-held policy that
women weren't allowed to go on the road with the band,
Willie said, "She's not a girl. She's a piano player."

My piano playing also underwent a change. For years I'd
worked as a soloist. Even when Freddy played drums behind
me at Dutchman's, his was a supportive role. Now all that
was changed. Now *I* was in a supportive role. I had to figure
out how my piano could fit into Willie's overall sound.

I remember the first gig. It was at John T. Floore's Country
Store in Helotes, Texas, outside San Antonio. Willie had made
John T. famous when he wrote about him in "Shotgun Wil-
lie," singing, "John T. Floore was working with the Ku Klux
Klan, the six-foot-five John T. was a helluva man, made a lot
of money selling sheets on the family plan."

The Country Store is an old-fashioned barn-size honky-
tonk. It took me back to the days when Willie and I were with
Bud Fletcher. I remember Bud telling me, "If you see a fight

break out or hear a gunshot, duck under the piano and stay there." No rough stuff that first night at John T.'s, but a very rough piano. Half the keys were missing. When I voiced a complaint, John T. said, "Most country bands don't use no piano. Do the best you can." I did just that.

John T. was the exception. Most venues had halfway-decent pianos, and as time went on and Willie became more popular, he bought me a new piano to take on the road. That meant I had a fine working instrument every night. Playing an in-tune instrument is something I never take for granted.

My main challenge in this new musical format was being heard. That meant playing louder. Hitting those keys with greater force. Letting the guys know I was here and had something to say. When I did so, Willie looked back and smiled. When he sang ballads, I could play little lyrical flourishes that hopefully inspired him. When the band went into "Whiskey River," I could find spaces in the hot rhythm to add my spice. And when, at the end of the show, we played a gospel song, it brought back memories of Abbott and my heart sang with joy.

The other seismic change was the crowds. I was used to upscale cocktail bars, elegant dinner clubs, or nice family restaurants. For nearly twenty years, that was my comfort zone. Willie pushed me out of that zone. Honky-tonks were nothing new, but more and more we were playing hippie palaces like the Armadillo.

We played the Austin Opry House on South Congress so often they called it the Willie Hilton. The dance hall section of the complex held two thousand fans. Weed was everywhere. A while back, I'd watched Willie switch out liquor for pot and was impressed by the difference. I hated whiskey for all the misery it caused people in my life. Pot caused no misery. Pot took off the edge and made Willie mellow. I started taking a few hits myself. I liked the effect. When it came to pot smoking, I could never match Willie—literally no one can—but I did experience the benefits. Anxiety softened. Anger erased. Music was made to sound even more haunting. As a high-strung person, I found pot to be a relaxant. And even in these psychedelic-centric venues we played, with the hippies tripping on LSD and the hillbillies buzzed on beer, I was never nervous. Willie found a cool that calmed down the scene while still exciting the crowd with his own brand of music.

BROTHER

They talked about the culture wars and the generation gap, but I didn't view the world that way. I watched the film of the Monterey International Pop Festival where soul singer Otis Redding asks the hordes of hippies who've come to see him, "This is the love crowd, right? We love each other, don't we?"

The answer was yes. That's the answer I always got when I went into a concert hall where the Grateful Dead had played the night before. I got love. And did my level best to give love back in return. I remember Waylon Jennings being nervous about playing the 'Dillo in Austin. This was sometime in the early seventies. Commander Cody was the opening act, and Waylon was sure the counterculture crowd wouldn't accept him. I was sure they would. He didn't believe me and started talking about walking.

"No worries, Waylon. They'll love you."

"Well, I ain't putting no flowers in my hair."

"You can put the flowers up your backside. Just get out there."

That night he went over big. Austin loved Waylon—and Merle Haggard and Johnny Cash—just as much as they loved me. When it came to music, there was no discrimination in Austin. Labels didn't matter. Whether it was club owner Clifford Antone bringing in Muddy Waters from Chicago to play with guitarist Jimmie Vaughan or Captain Beefheart jamming at Threadgill's, Austin greeted music makers with open arms. It was musical democracy. Just good songs sung by good singers played by good bands.

YOU MIGHT REMEMBER that, even as a kid, I was promoting, booking Bob Wills at Lake Whitney. My promoter streak stayed strong. In '73 it had me dreaming of the idea of a Fourth of July Woodstock-styled picnic festival in Dripping Springs, Texas. My partner was Leon Russell. He said, "You bring the rednecks, Willie, and I'll bring the hippies."

I liked Leon's attitude. I also liked Leon's company. He was a serious musician who didn't take the music business all that seriously. That doesn't mean he didn't like to make money—who doesn't like money?—but he also knew that the music business was straitlaced and ultraconservative. Only a guy like Leon would be willing to take a chance on this crazy picnic idea.

Anticipation was high. Fact is, the night before, we got high and never got to sleep. Can't say for sure, but maybe, in spite of our outward confidence, deep down we were a little scared that no one would show up. Smoking calmed our nerves. So did music. So when night turned to day, Leon and I walked onto the empty stage and started fooling around with old gospel hymns, him on piano, me on guitar. Must have been playing a good hour when, way off on the horizon, we saw a few folks straggling into the picnic grounds. They looked a little lost.

"Well," said Leon, "if we only get a dozen people, those dozen people are gonna hear the show of their lives."

"Amen."

Leon and I kept playing to that small crowd. An hour later, a few more fans showed up. Finally, a slow stream turned into a roaring river and—lo and behold—the grounds were packed. Half the crowd were hippies, half were rednecks, but all full-blooded music lovers. Those rednecks and hippies brought their brothers and sisters and mothers and fathers and aunts and uncles plus all their neighbors and friends. The stars who performed came from both sides of the galaxy, Loretta Lynn, Rita Coolidge, Waylon Jennings, Asleep at the Wheel, Charlie Rich, Kris Kristofferson, Ernest Tubb. We couldn't have been more unorganized. We couldn't have had more fun. Who knew that Willie's Picnic would turn into a yearly event for the next forty-six years?

In this same time zone, I'd written a suite of songs about a couple's divorce—half the tunes written from the man's perspective, the other half from the woman's—when Jerry Wexler popped up again. Every time Jerry popped up, he had a new idea. This time he wanted me to record these songs in Muscle Shoals, where Wilson Pickett and Aretha had cut hits. When Jerry's colleague said, "Muscle Shoals is too R&B for Willie," Wexler shot back, "Willie's too R&B for Nashville." I called the record *Phases and Stages.* The big single, released in 1974, was "Bloody Mary Morning," something I'd written in my pre-pot days. The saddest song by far was "I Still Can't Believe You're Gone," about Carlene English, the wife of my drummer, Paul, who died tragically. Her passing nearly killed Paul as well. This song was the strongest form of sympathy I could offer.

SISTER

Willie's a true artist, and true artists experiment. They experiment with their minds and their music. That's why I wasn't especially surprised to learn that Willie was wanting to take LSD. He thought it would expand his consciousness. He said we were living in the Age of Aquarius and he didn't want to be left out of any of the spiritual fun. I had offers to do the same, but being more cautious than Brother, I stuck with an occasional hit of pot and an after-the-show glass of wine.

Before Willie took the acid, I asked him whether he was sure it was a good idea. We had a show in a couple of hours. He told me that this pure stuff came from a chemist in San Francisco. He had no fear. That's Willie. Well, instead of taking a third of the tab, he mistakenly took the whole thing—fifteen hundred micrograms instead of five hundred. Right off, he seemed fine. Lots of smiles, smooth sailing ahead. But then I could see things change. When it came close to show-time, he had trouble holding his guitar. He started hallucinating. Because Bee, Mickey, Paul, and I knew that something was wrong, we slowed down the rhythms and made sure Willie got through the songs okay. Afterward, we surrounded him, enclosing him in a circle of love. I didn't see panic in his eyes, but I did know he was eager for the trip to end. It took almost all night for him to come down, and we never left his side. The next day he slept till the afternoon. When he woke up, his first words didn't surprise me: "Never again."

Brother *is* an experimenter, but he also knows himself. He knew that for other people LSD might well open their minds and let them escape their egos. Willie and I both loved Eastern philosophy that talked about getting beyond your ego to join the Oneness of cosmic consciousness. I think he had the notion that acid might help bring about that consciousness. When it didn't, he swore it off. He stuck with pot, his tried-and-true friend that he began to consider as much a medicine as a relaxant. He learned all about marijuana and its healing and practical uses. He became a pioneer in championing the substance. He backed political candidates running on a let's-legalize-pot platform. It became Willie's personal crusade, and now, nearly fifty years later, we can look back and see that he was right. The world has finally caught up with Willie.

BROTHER

When Atlantic Records closed down their Nashville office, Jerry Wexler was worried the label couldn't properly support me. Despite our close bond, we both knew I'd do better elsewhere. That's when I signed with the biggest record company in the world, Columbia, with the one condition I'd learned from Jerry—I had to have creative control.

At about the time Columbia met my terms, it was 1974 and Connie and I went skiing in Colorado. On the drive out there, Connie reminded me of that old song "Redheaded Stranger" I used to play and dedicate to my daughter Lana when I was working as a deejay in Fort Worth. That got me to thinking of other old tunes I loved, like Fred Rose's "Blue Eyes Crying in the Rain." A little later Sister asked me if I remembered "Just As I Am," a hymn we sang back in Abbott. Sure, I did.

Back from Colorado, I had Mickey Raphael find an out-of-the-way studio for us to record at. Turned out to be Autumn Sound in Garland, Texas, a burb of Dallas. I went old-school. Used my own band. I recorded the way Eddy Arnold used to record. One or two takes. Of the $60,000 recording budget Columbia allotted me, I spent $2,000. I used the other $58,000 to buy new equipment and instruments for my band.

When the label heard it, they thought it was a demo. Too rough, too sparse. Go to Nashville. Use the studio musicians. Polish it up. I listened but didn't budge. Simply pointed to the contract that said I could do what I wanted. I wanted it released as is. It was heartfelt and direct. Heartfelt and direct was my intention. *Red Headed Stranger,* as unpolished as it was, went gold. "Blue Eyes Crying in the Rain" went number one. That $2,000 session sent my career soaring in a whole new direction. I didn't give up the big honky-tonk venues and never will, but I did find myself standing on stages with symphony orchestras accompanying me as I sang "Crazy" and "Funny How Time Slips Away." One night I was facing an audience wearing suits and gowns, the next night folks in overalls and Daisy Mae cutoff jeans.

SISTER

Funny how names kept bumping into each other. First there was Bud Fletcher. Then there was Bud Smith. Now here comes Jack Fletcher. No relation to Bud, Jack was Paul English's running buddy. They'd both come up together in Fort Worth. They were both tough guys devoted to protecting their friends at any cost. In Paul's case, that friend was Willie. And in Jack's case, that friend—and lover—was me.

I can look back now with a clarity that I lacked in the seventies when Jack and I became a couple. My life was radically changed. My sons were independent. Michael had graduated from law school. Randy and Freddy were in Austin, stable, happy, and productive. I could go out on the road with Willie and not have to worry. For Willie, the road is endless. He thrives on the road. He's been wandering off since he was a little boy. Wandering off is just his nature. It feeds his restless spirit. It's also part of the reason he has enjoyed such amazing longevity as a star. He stays close to his fans, not simply through his records but also through his shows. He wants to be with his fans, and his fans want to be with him.

Now I was part of that phenomenon. Not that I was anything close to being a star or even had a wish to be one. Willie had star power enough for everyone. But as a permanent member of Family, I had an obligation. No more getting to the supper club at 5:00 P.M. and leaving at 11:00. Willie's work meant travel, travel, travel. Rejoining Brother as his musical playmate made it more than worthwhile, but a big adjustment was required. I was the only woman in the band. And the idea of having a companion, someone who was with me virtually all the time, had strong appeal.

I had met Jack years earlier when I was playing Randolph Air Force Base in San Antonio. He came through with Willie and Paul. I was attracted to him. He was six feet tall, a nice-looking man dressed in a suit and tie. Paul had brought him into Willie's entourage as security. Jack and I spoke briefly. I felt the sparks. I believe he did, too, but at that point nothing happened.

It wasn't until a year later when I had begun traveling the world with Willie that Jack came back into the picture. He had changed his clean-cut look. Instead of a suit and tie, he wore overalls. He'd grown a beard and, along with most everyone else, was smoking pot. This time around things got serious. I actually initiated the romance by asking him out for coffee. He liked my artistic spirit. I liked his take-charge attitude. We fell in love. It proved to be a difficult love. Even in the beginning the signs were there—he had a short temper and hung out with some shady characters—but I chose to ignore them.

Jack and I were together on the road and also in Austin. He moved in with me. The first alarming episode involved my German shepherd police dog, Kaiser. I've always loved dogs. One day I came home and found Kaiser lying on our front lawn, lifeless. I rushed him to the vet, who said he had been poisoned. I learned that Jack was embroiled in a blood feud with a rough crowd who had killed Kaiser in retribution for something that Jack and his friends may have done. The loss of my dog was devastating. And also frightening. It made me feel that, even more, I needed protection. Strangely, this early incident may have brought me closer to Jack because Jack was my protector, even as I understood that he was hardly an upstanding citizen.

Our bond was intimate. Our bond may well have been based on my fear of being alone. Whatever brought us together, though, was powerful. I say that because, in spite of increasingly questionable behavior on Jack's part, we stayed together. For too long.

Far too long.

BROTHER

Having Bobbie in the band changed the course of my music in more ways than most people understand. Sometimes she and I would be at rehearsals by ourselves and she'd start playing standards. No one knows more standards than Bobbie. Even before she started playing at high-class bistros, she had a vast knowledge of the Great American Songbook from Stephen Foster to George Gershwin. She could play "Beautiful Dreamer," she could play "Summertime." Sister could play anything. Having her around me again, day in and out, reminded me of how much I loved those songs. No matter how obscure a tune might be, I could mention it to Bobbie and she'd play it from top to bottom.

One night we were reminiscing when she happened to say that the first standard she learned—the one she loved best—was "Stardust." I love the song and started humming it. I didn't remember the lyrics, so I got the sheet music and began singing it. I asked Bobbie what other songs she thought might work for an album devoted to favorites from the past. She gave me a list that included "All of Me," "Moonlight in Vermont," "Blue Skies," "Someone to Watch Over Me," and "September Song."

By happenstance, Connie, the girls, and I were living in Malibu the summer of 1977, and Booker T. Jones and his wife had a place in the same complex. I knew him from his great band, Booker T. and the MG's. I didn't know, though, that Booker was also a fine arranger and producer. One afternoon I was hanging out in his apartment, where he had a battery of keyboards. I mentioned my idea about singing standards. He encouraged me and thought he could help. We both agreed to keep things simple. Didn't need strings. Didn't need background singers. Didn't need horns. Use my own crew—Bee on bass, Paul on drums, Mickey on harmonica, Sister on piano, Jody Payne on guitar. My only reservation was about singing "Georgia on My Mind." By then Ray Charles and I had become good buddies. His version of the old song was already a classic. When I mentioned to Ray that I might sing it, wondering about his reaction, he was quick to say, "Sure you should sing the thing, Willie. I wasn't the first to do it, and you won't be the last. These songs don't belong to us. They belong to the world."

We cut the whole album in a week.

SISTER

One of the things that makes me proudest about my brother is his integrity. Especially with music. When we got through recording *Stardust,* we were thrilled. Willie gave those old songs new life. But then we heard that the record company wasn't happy. Willie's previous album, *Red Headed Stranger,* was a big hit. Then he was part of *Wanted! The Outlaws,* a compilation with Waylon Jennings, Tompall Glaser, and Jessi Colter, the first platinum-certified album in country music history. Outlaw Country was all the rage, and Brother was right in the middle of the mix. To cash in, Columbia Records wanted an outlaw album, not a record that nostalgically looked back at songs popular in previous decades.

But Willie stood his ground. Willie always stands his ground. He said, "If a song was a hit once, it can be a hit again."

The business music is all about trends. Willie is all about good music.

It wasn't that the outlaw label bothered him. In some ways that description did fit both him and Waylon. They both had gone against the Nashville establishment. And they both had reached broad audiences, young and old, in a style different from country artists who came before them.

But Willie wasn't about to be put in a box or made to conform to what music executives thought the public wanted.

Willie had earned his creative freedom. Once he had it, he wasn't about to let it go.

Observing how Willie ignored the so-called marketing experts and made the music he wanted, I was tickled to death. All these big shots running around trying to figure out how to make the most money. Meanwhile, Brother was happy simply making music. Money came, money went, but the music stayed.

BROTHER

Standing in front of the Abbott Methodist Church, 1978

In 1978, I turned forty-five, Sister turned forty-seven, and life seemed to be going our way. Our musical reunion had borne fruit. Having her back in the band proved that I was right about her all along. She was the missing piece of my musical puzzle. Having her onstage every night meant we'd be singing gospel songs at evening's end. I loved it.

I took Connie and the girls and moved out to Colorado for a spell. Thought the clear mountain air would do me good. It did. But being a wanderer, I didn't settle down for long. Unexpectedly, Hollywood came a-calling. No way I wasn't gonna answer that call. If my heroes Gene Autry and Roy Rogers could be cowboys in movies, well, I'd give it a go. Worst thing that could happen would be falling off a horse. But I'm a good rider. Staying in the saddle was something I could handle. I could also handle film roles like playing Robert Redford's manager in *The Electric Horseman.* My character in *Honeysuckle Rose* was Buck Bonham, half in love with my wife, Dyan Cannon, and half in love with my girlfriend, Amy Irving. The directors let me play myself. Good thing, because that's about all I could do. For the Buck Bonham movie I wrote a simple little song called "On the Road Again." Truest and simplest song I ever wrote.

Still singing it.

Got a little tired of the Rockies and, true to my nature, moved home to Texas. Bought me a beat-up country club called the Pedernales in the town of Spicewood in the hills outside Austin with lots of land attached, including a rough and rocky golf course. Didn't mind the pebbles and stones. Countryside was pretty. Close to where the Pedernales River spills into Lake Travis. It was the perfect spot to build a recording studio, and that's what I did. Lots of peace and quiet. Great place to be creative. Named the whole thing Luck Ranch 'cause I liked to say, "When you're here, you're in Luck, and when you're not, you're out of Luck."

I haven't declared many mandates in my life save for a few. When it came to drugs, especially cocaine, I said, "If you're wired, you're fired." Pot was a calm-you-down mellow-you-out. Coke was a fire-you-up make-you-nuts. Second mandate applied to Pedernales. No killing nothing. No shooting deer, wild ducks, geese, or turtles. No rabbit hunting. Don't even harm a grasshopper. Eventually I was able to fence off a big ol' pasture where more than seventy horses, rescued from slaughter, could get hand-fed twice a day and graze till their hearts' content. No one can tell me that horses don't have souls.

SISTER

At the end of 1978, our father died of lung cancer. It wasn't an easy death. He was only sixty-five. Even though he was closer to Willie than to me, I loved him. I appreciated how Willie kept him in our lives. I don't think he and Willie had a single disagreement. I love the memory of his joining our first band with Bud Fletcher, and I love how he forged a relationship with my own sons.

A year later, the death of Mama Nelson was an even bigger blow. She had spent her last years in a nursing community in Fort Worth. Though she lived a long life, the loss was devastating. The woman was my heart. She raised us. Single-handedly. She saw me through every crisis. She stayed steady; she stayed faithful; she loved the Lord with such conviction that no one who knew her doubted her devotion. Without Mama Nelson, I wouldn't be here telling my story. I borrowed her strength. I leaned on her loyalty.

Daddy was musical, but it was Mama Nelson who really made sure that Willie and I took music seriously. To our great fortune, she was a teacher and we her prized students. We loved the hymns she taught us, but even when Willie and I went far afield and started playing barrooms and honky-tonks, she never criticized. She understood that the spirit of music is stronger than any single genre. She knew that

Brother and I would be making people happy and carrying a good message, no matter where we might be performing. Mama Nelson had deep wisdom. She shepherded us in a way that no one else could have. She was never driven by self-interest. She was driven solely, purely by love. She covered and protected us with a love that I feel as strongly today as I did eighty years ago when, as a small girl, this remarkable woman placed my hands on the keys of a piano.

MAMA NELSON DIED at the very end of the seventies. I didn't know it then, but the eighties would become by far the most difficult decade of my life. My grandmother wasn't there to see me through. It was the God she taught me to love that saw me through. It was her God-informed spirit that I relied on. Yet even with that spirit, even with that loving God, I came close to losing my mind. Never before in life had I faced catastrophes of such dimension.

PART VI

THE STORY OF LOSS...

BROTHER

On the road in Delaware, the eighties

With Bobbie in Family and playing on most of our records, I had success in the eighties. We found new fans and, inspired by a comment by Bob Dylan, I started Farm Aid with John Mellencamp and Neil Young. Thirty-five years later, it's still going strong. It's been a great way to focus on helping American farmers.

My career found a momentum of its own. Our records kept selling. Our shows kept selling out. Many blessings came my way.

In 1983, we lost our mother. Like Dad, Mom died of lung cancer. I hate how tobacco poisoned both my parents. I was lucky to swear it off early, but I wish I could have convinced them both to do the same. Both their deaths were agonizing. At the end of her life, Mom was living in Yakima in Washington State and, until the cancer hit, she always kept her spirits high. Her high spirits are part of my DNA, and I thank her for that. She was a character, a strong independent lady way ahead of her time. Bobbie and I loved how she'd unexpectedly pop up in our lives. A couple of times—once at Caesars Palace in Vegas and then again in Houston—she appeared onstage and sang along with us as we broke into "Up Against the Wall, Redneck Mother." She was funny and spunky and satisfied that, with the great help of her in-laws, her daughter and son had made something of themselves. Bless her memory.

On the romantic front, I still hadn't really reformed. I messed up another marriage. My wandering ways were too much for any woman to put up with. I'll always love Connie. I'll always love all my wives. I've always said that there's no such thing as a "former" wife. Once in your life, a wife never leaves. I regret the pain I caused Connie—and Martha and Shirley before her—and have no excuses.

But love is love, and in the mideighties I fell head over heels in love with Ann Marie D'Angelo, called Annie. Never had met a woman like her before. She was a makeup artist on *Stagecoach,* a movie I was doing with Waylon, Kris Kristofferson, and Johnny Cash. The four of us had formed the Highwaymen and over the next ten years would cut three albums and tour the world. Working with friends I admired so deeply was a tremendous privilege, not to mention big fun. We were all different and yet the same. Johnny was more on the conservative side; Kris more liberal; Waylon was, well, Waylon;

and I'm not sure I belong in any category. Our sameness had to do with our love of music—music of all kinds—and our love for each other. Fans felt that love and supported us from start to finish.

My love for Annie was all-consuming, but winning her over wasn't easy. She had to be sure my marriage was over and that I was truly free. She didn't care about me being a celebrity. She was whip-smart, with a keen appreciation for all forms of art. It didn't hurt that she was pretty and radiated enough energy to light up any room she entered. She also had a sharp political sense. Later she'd be a great partner in pushing the progressive causes so important to me.

You've already seen that, when it came to romance, I had a gift for complicating things. But marrying Annie wasn't complicated at all. It's about the smartest thing I ever did. I can say that because, thirty-four years after we first met, we're still together and going strong.

But as beautiful as this romance was, it came at a time when Sister was going through something none of us saw coming. I was there for her. The whole family was. We rallied around Bobbie. But no matter how much support we gave, nothing could really soften the blows.

What happened would have destroyed most women. But Bobbie ain't most women.

Bobbie is Bobbie.

SISTER

Freddy, Michael, and Randy, 1988

I need to take a big sigh. I need to close my eyes, catch my breath, gather up strength. I need to steel my nerves and stay steady. This isn't an easy story to tell.

It would be easier if my relationship with Jack Fletcher had gone better. But it hadn't. We never married but were together for some fifteen years. I made many mistakes. The first was allowing Jack to get into my money. By show business standards, I was not superrich, but staying on the road with Willie had provided me with a good income. I'm not an extravagant spender and believe in putting something aside for a rainy day. But I'm also—or at least I was—an old-fashioned woman conditioned to let the man lead the way. In Jack's case, that was a mistake. Jack was far too proprietary about my finances. When it came to my money, he was aggressive. He considered it his. I gave up control when I should not have. Our long-term live-in situation meant that we had, in fact, a common-law marriage. My attorney friend Joel Mitchell urged me to separate my finances and property from Jack's. I knew that was a wise course of action, but I was afraid to do so. I thought it might destroy my relationship. I was too weak to challenge Jack.

To admit that a man had me under his thumb isn't easy. As I write this, I want to appear stronger than I was. But the reality is that I was intimidated. Jack was a forceful character. He had gangster proclivities. Had I been a different person, I would have gotten away from him much earlier than I did. Yet the truth is that I loved him. He had a strength that made me feel safe, even if the feeling was an illusion.

As it turned out, it took the illness that befell my son Michael to force me into doing what I should have done years earlier.

After graduating from Memphis State with a law degree, Michael moved to Los Angeles, where he became a successful entertainment lawyer. He was doing beautifully. He was much beloved by his clients and colleagues. At first, he worked for a major law firm run by Jerry Milliken, a mentor to Michael. Soon Milliken had Michael heading an entire division. Eventually Michael opened his own office. He was prospering and making his mother proud. He always stayed close to me and his brothers, Randy and Freddy.

Girls adored him. But back in law school, when one of his male friends died a tragically young death, I did observe how

Michael's mourning was especially deep. I suspected that the young man had been more to Michael than simply a friend. The fact that my son might be gay didn't bother me except for one thing: I didn't want him to suffer discrimination. I had felt the heavy weight of discrimination when the Hill County judge condemned me for being a female piano player. That was double discrimination—against me as a woman and against the idea of entertaining in honky-tonks. Then during my years with Jesse Oriana we were always facing ugly prejudice. We tried to ignore it—and, for the most part, we did—but it was an emotional burden.

Gay people have always had to deal with vicious discrimination. If I was hoping my son wasn't gay, it was only because I wanted to spare him pain. I don't judge homosexuality or bisexuality. Those are natural. But society does judge, and society is cruel. I didn't want Michael to have to bear society's bias. I didn't want him being scorned as an outcast or misfit.

As the years went by, though, it seemed clear that Michael's earlier relationships with the opposite sex had not blossomed into romance. There were no longer any girl-friends. He and I never discussed it. Nor did Michael mention it to his brothers. His private life was his private life. It was only when we learned that he was in the hospital in Los Angeles that everything changed. When I talked to him, he said it was nothing serious. But then toward the end of 1986, Randy, sensing that it might be worse than Michael let on, went out to see him. The minute he returned to Austin, Randy called to say that I needed to fly out to L.A. Michael needed his mother.

That's when I learned Michael had been diagnosed with AIDS. He was HIV positive. In those days many AIDS patients were denied admittance to regular hospitals, and Michael had gone to a special facility. When I saw him, I was stunned. He had lost a great deal of weight. Something was terribly wrong. The doctors explained the gravity of the disease. As they spoke, I found it hard to breathe. All I knew was that I needed to keep my composure. I needed to be strong. Michael needed support. I had to be there for him.

His brothers and I rallied around him. During that initial trip to L.A., I met Michael's partner, Tony Bugato, a great guy who loved my son with all his heart. It comforted me to learn that my son was in a nurturing relationship. Tony's response was the same as ours—to comfort Michael. We contacted other doctors, specialists, and researchers. We learned all we could. This was during the Reagan administration, when the government was horribly negligent. They never prioritized a cure. One of the president's press secretaries even joked about it, calling it the "gay plague." When it came to AIDS, we were still in the Dark Ages.

Michael was thirty-four. He was stoic. He said he would do whatever he had to do to fight for his life. I said I would fight alongside him. I left Austin to stay with him in Los Angeles. I told Willie I'd need time off, and Willie gave his full support.

I didn't discuss Michael's condition, but Jack found out. When he did, our relationship fell apart.

"I don't want you around Michael," he said. "And I sure as hell won't let him near me."

"I don't understand."

"He's contagious."

"You can't catch AIDS by being in the same room with someone."

"Says who?"

"Says his doctors. The experts have proven you can only catch it through intimate contact."

"I don't believe the experts."

"Look, Jack, if you think I'm abandoning my son, you're crazy."

"Risk your own life if you want to, but I ain't risking mine."

Jack's ugly attitude shocked and infuriated me. He was talking about my son. My baby boy. In the fifteen years we'd been together, I'd never gone against Jack. I let him lead. But no more. When he told me that I couldn't go to Los Angeles to be with Michael, I paid him no mind. I just walked out the door.

Michael's ordeal lasted three years. His deterioration was a horrific process. I refrain from detailing that deterioration only because to do so is too painful. I watched my poor baby go through hell. Jack was making everything even harder. He was afraid that the end of our relationship would mean the end of his gravy train. He never stopped pushing his insane argument that you can catch AIDS by merely being in the same surroundings as an AIDS patient. He did everything he could to separate me from Michael and Michael's needs. He even tried to drive a wedge between me and Willie. But no one in the world could ever do that. In no uncertain terms, Willie let Jack know that he supported me and his nephew in every possible way.

As Michael grew worse, I decided to move him to Austin. That got Jack even crazier while making me even more determined. Jack hated how I was spending money—money he considered half his—on my son. Jack also wouldn't even enter the same room as Michael. Meanwhile, Randy, who was in real estate, arranged to buy a house for Michael in Briarcliff, a little town near Willie's ranch outside Austin. I paid for it but put the house in Michael's name. I did that to block

Jack's claim that, due to our common-law marriage, half of my property belonged to him.

I continued to keep this private. This was during the time that Willie had split up with Connie and met Annie. He'd bought property in Maui, and when he wasn't on the road, he was in Hawaii a great deal of the time. Willie had so much going on. Besides, I felt strong enough to deal with it. Michael's condition brought out a newfound confidence in myself. I could handle this. For the sake of my precious son, I would stay steady. Not a thing in the world could stop that.

Randy and Freddy were with me every step of the way. Willie knew what I was going through, but there was only so much he could do. He said I could rejoin the band whenever I thought that might bring me relief. There were times, in fact, when that did bring me relief. Playing a show now and then took my mind off my son's crisis, at least for a few hours.

At one point, to be closer to the hospital, I bought a condo in downtown Austin that I shared with Michael. When Jack found out, he went ballistic. He saw what he considered his money going down the drain. One day when Michael and I were at the hospital, Jack hired someone to ransack the condo. That was the final blow. My friend Joel Mitchell stepped in and set up legal protections so that Jack could no longer touch my money. At long last, he was out of my life.

The last days of Michael's life were brutal. If I could, I would erase those memories from my mind. But I can't. The nightmare was too real to ever forget. What I can do, though, is turn to happier thoughts. I can remember those afternoons and evenings when Michael was still strong enough to walk next door with me to the Four Seasons. He loved that hotel. We'd have brunch there. Often Randy, his wife, Phyllis, and Freddy would join us for dinner. The Four Seasons became our refuge, our sanctuary, a place where I could see a glimmer of hope in Michael's eyes. We would hold hands. We would speak of happy times on Willie's Ridgetop farm, the times Michael would have dinner at Dutchman's and watch me and his brother Freddy play the songs that everyone, including Michael, loved so dearly.

Dear Michael was stalwart. Dear Michael was strong. He was sweet. He was brilliant. Even in the fading light of his life, he never failed to express his gratitude. His kindness only grew. His goodness only deepened. In 1989, three years after his diagnosis, we lost him. I lost him.

But we never really lost him. Great spirits don't die. I feel Michael's spirit now. He is as close to me as he has ever been. He is my son, a gift from God. I keep him close.

BROTHER

The death of my nephew Michael was the saddest day in Sister's life. Her son was a special man whose whole life was in front of him. The loss was too great for any of us to ever imagine. But then came another loss just as brutal. Or maybe even more brutal because it came on the heels of Michael's passing.

I don't know how Bobbie survived it. But she did. In her life, she's survived more than anyone I know.

SISTER

Bobbie, daughter-in-law Lisa, Michael (seated), Freddy, Randy, and daughter-in-law Phyllis, Austin, 1988

There's no way to compare how the loss of a loved one impacts family members. A mother's grief in losing a child, a brother's grief in losing a sibling, a man's grief in losing a loving partner, an uncle's grief in losing a nephew—everyone suffers in ways that defy description. Our family was devastated. But looking back, it's clear that the devastation impacted my son Randy the most.

As a child, Randy was closest to his father, Bud. As the oldest, Randy got to know Bud best. He was eleven when his dad died. That traumatized him. I've been told that in the aftermath of trauma, anxiety can assault you for the rest of your life. Randy suffered from shattered nerves. Marrying Phyllis was the best thing that happened to him. She helped stabilize him and for a long while he was doing well. But his brother's death proved too much.

On the day that Michael passed, Randy collapsed in the hospital room. Emotionally, he fell apart. The people closest to him—Freddy, Phyllis, and me—did all we could. We took him to doctors who prescribed psychotropic medicines that didn't work. I believe, if anything, the meds made him worse. I understand that antidepressants don't always work. Thirty years ago, there was far less sophistication about such medicines than there is now. But even today I'm told that psychiatrists continue to struggle with finding the right combination of medicines to treat erratic behavior.

Randy never found the right combination. Oh, how he struggled! Like so many other people who deal with mental illness, he went on meds, only to go off the meds, only to go on again. Making matters worse, he began drinking heavily. I tried to reach him, console him, calm him down. Everyone tried, but my son was out of control.

I lived in fear for his safety.

Like most mothers, I'm fiercely protective. Like most mothers, I'd give my own life to save any of my children. And like most mothers, I've suffered the most when I've realized that all I had done to help save my son was not enough. That realization came first with Michael. Then it came again with Randy.

On the night before January 1, 1990, my fifty-ninth birthday, Randy was killed in a car wreck. On New Year's Eve, he was driving on Farm Road 1431 in Marble Falls, a little town outside Austin. The winding two-lane highway is perilous under the best conditions. It's notorious for fatal accidents. Randy lost control of the car and ran off the road. He was alone. No one else was injured. By the time an ambulance arrived, he was gone. He was thirty-nine.

In a period of six months, I had lost two sons. I reach for words that are not there. No song is sad enough to express the pain. After Michael, I thought I knew grief. I did not imagine how grief could grow any deeper. The death of Randy taught me that it could. I was covered in grief. I was drowning in grief. I was numb. Freddy, Phyllis, Willie, Annie—my family stayed by my side, got me through the funeral, attended to my every need.

And yet the grief could not be abated. My beautiful boys. The grief continues.

BROTHER

I suppose the mix of joy and pain is what life's all about. We try to focus on joy but there's no way to escape the pain. Seems like the start of the nineties was a time like no other. The joy was incredible, yet so was the pain.

The joy of being with Annie was a beautiful thing. Our first son, Lukas, was born in 1988, followed two years later by Micah. Pure bliss.

From 1985 to 1995, touring the world with the Highwaymen was also a happy time. You'd think it'd be hard for ornery guys like me, Waylon, Kris, and Johnny to get along. But it wasn't. We grew closer. We laughed louder. Our band got tighter. Our music got better. Our young kids played together. Our wives bonded. Our merry gang rolled 'round the world, each gig more fun than the last.

I made some mistakes. Always have and always will. I had the idea that Annie and I would raise Lukas and Micah the way I was raised. I bought the house of Doc Simms, the physician who brought Bobbie and me into the world, and moved us all back to Abbott. The local folk were fine. They were glad to have me home and respected our privacy. But somehow word got 'round and people from all over would find their way to Abbott and, uninvited, come knocking at our door. When I was home, I could politely sign a few autographs and send them on their way. But when I was on the road and Annie was alone with the boys, it got to be too much. Once, in the middle of a peaceful night in Abbott, a drunk rammed his pickup into our porch and started screaming for me. When that happened, I was playing out in California. Understandably, the incident shook up Annie. We kept Doc Simms's house but moved back to Austin.

More mistakes: I bought a private jet that cost a fortune and proved to be a tougher way of getting around than the bus. Bad weather never stopped the bus the way it grounded the plane. Had to sell the thing at a loss.

Also tried leasing Mel Tillis's theater in Branson, Missouri. I figured Annie, the boys, and I could comfortably live in a big hotel suite for six months. That would cut down a lot of my time on the road. Make life more stable. Well, it made life hell. At the time Branson had no infrastructure. The city was a mess and it didn't take me long to realize how I hated staying in the same place for so long. I was—and am—a road dog. We headed back to Austin, where the boys were raised on the ranch and also at our home in Maui.

Then came the lowest point. I said before that I couldn't imagine suffering the pain that Bobbie suffered when she lost two of her sons. In 1991, I didn't have to imagine it. It became stark reality. I lost my beautiful son Billy, then only thirty-three, in a terrible accident. Our family was still reeling from what happened to Michael and Randy. Now Billy, another talented young man, died decades before his time.

All my children—Lana, Susie, Billy, Paula, Amy, Lukas, and Micah—mean the world. Another one of my children was Renee, born to Mary—the woman I'd been with in Waco back when I was a teenager—and given up for adoption. She came back into my life, and I welcomed her with open arms. Renee became part of our family. After her passing, her children and grandchildren have remained in our lives.

The loving memory of my son Billy still lives with me every day.

SISTER

Filming a gospel video at the chapel in Luck, Texas, 1993

I love the Psalms. I derive comfort when I read Psalm 33, which talks about those who rely on God's "unfailing love." Because our lives are so filled with unspeakable pain and unimaginable loss, we all need something that's "unfailing." At least I do.

In the nineties, after the passing of Michael, Randy, and Billy, Willie and I grew even closer. It wasn't that we had long talks about our grief. That's not Willie's way. We didn't have to talk about it. We knew. We had shared so much in our childhood that had bonded us—our parents leaving, Daddy Nelson dying, the fear of being separated from Mama Nelson—that we were already attuned to each other's heart. The fact that we both experienced shattering loss as adults only intensified our understanding. I knew what Willie was going through. He knew how I was suffering. And the mere fact of being together made the burden a little lighter.

Willie never stopped making records. Because his imagination is so vast, some of those albums were big productions with lush strings and intense orchestrations. On other records he sang beautiful duets with Bonnie Raitt, Paul Simon, and Bob Dylan. Everyone wanted to sing with Willie. But in the midnineties, there came a change. Willie and I played a show in Santa Fe—just the two of us—that was a big success. It was the first time we'd ever done that. Naturally it took us both back to our childhood. Many of the songs we included were the hymns that Mama Nelson had taught us. All that got Willie to thinking about doing a simple album. No outside producer. No big arrangements. We cut it in his Pedernales studio. It was a religious experience. It helped provide the relief that Brother and I so desperately needed. He wrote original songs for the sessions that unfolded in a beautifully natural way. Appropriately enough, Willie called the album *Spirit*.

BROTHER

*Bobbie with her only grandchild (and look-alike), Ellee,
at Willie and Annie's cabin, 2015*

Spirit was necessary—necessary for Bobbie and necessary for me. I've always said that Sister's abiding faith washes over me. It was Bobbie's faith that inspired me to write a song I called "I Thought About You, Lord."

I thought about trees
And how much I'd like to climb one

I thought about friends
And how rare it is to find one

I thought about you
The most gentle, sweet, and kind one
I thought about you, Lord
I thought about you

I thought about life
And the way that things are goin'
I thought about love
And the pain there is in growin'

And I thought about you
The one who is all-knowin'
I thought about you, Lord
I thought about you

I thought about you
And the songs that I keep singin'
I thought about you
And the joy that they keep bringin'

Looking back at these lyrics, I see them as a prayer. It's taken me a lifetime to realize that, in some sense, music has always been my form of praying. That makes sense because my first music in the Abbott Methodist United Church was prayer hymns. But going beyond that, going to songs of lost love or songs about angels flying too close to the ground, I see that my songs are how I express what otherwise wouldn't be expressed. That spirit aims to mend the broken heart.

The other songs from *Spirit* reflect the same feeling that Sister and I were sharing. One was called "I'm Not Trying to

Forget You Anymore." Another was "Too Sick to Pray." Then there was "I'm Waiting Forever" and "I Guess I've Come to Live Here in Your Eyes."

Johnny Gimble came in to play fiddle on a few songs, and Jody Payne brought his guitar, but the record was mainly a conversation between Bobbie and me. It was all about healing.

SISTER

I do believe that if Willie's music had stopped, if he had lost interest in making music or if his fans had lost interest in him, that might have been a fatal blow. But the opposite happened. Year after year, he got more famous and more beloved by music lovers everywhere. They wouldn't let him alone. They wouldn't let him *not* play. And playing music, for him and me, is the best medicine. I say that not only because we like to please people with songs, but also because those songs contain a spirit that keeps us positive.

Like Willie, I've read many different theologies and liked what I've read. What I've read, though, is no different than what I've always believed. Call it God, call it spirit, call it higher power. The words don't matter. What does matter is the thing itself. And that's love. When Willie and I are playing music, we're feeling, giving, and receiving love. That's what sustains us. And despite all we've endured, love, as expressed in music, is the core of everything.

Another inspiring example is the way Willie made it through another grueling crisis that hit him hard in the nineties. Claiming he owed $32 million in back taxes, the IRS took away virtually all his worldly possessions. It was front-page news. Willie Nelson lost his houses, his ranch, his studio, everything. Ironically, it wasn't even Willie's fault. The fault lay with a negligent accountant. Willie was blindsided by the whole thing. He was told he had to declare bankruptcy. But Brother wouldn't do that because he wasn't about to burn anyone he owed money to.

Willie did what Willie always does. He looked adversity dead in the eye and didn't blink. He held his head high. He fought back. He used the wit and wisdom he had cultivated over a lifetime. He went into the studio and made two great records—*The IRS Tapes* and *Who'll Buy My Memories.* Both sold like hotcakes. He used that money to satisfy the IRS and finally got himself back on firm financial footing. I was proud of him for standing tall. The way Willie overcame a crisis that would have crippled most men was flat-out amazing. He turned a low point into a high point, all the while keeping his cool. No temper tantrums, no vindictiveness. From then on, things got better.

BROTHER

Show business is one business that will make you crazy. If I avoided craziness, which I believe I have, it's only 'cause I've stayed true to the people who put me in the public eye. Ray Price was one of those people. When he hired me as his bassist—even though I couldn't play the damn thing— and I toured as a Cherokee Cowboy, I was in hog heaven. I love his version of "Night Life" more than my own. And so when my career was building up and his was going down, I made it a point to do a record with him called *Last of the Breed*. Merle Haggard was also part of that breed. He joined us in the studio. Less than ten years later when Ray Price died, I felt like I'd lost part of myself. I took my mourning into the studio and did *For the Good Times: A Tribute to Ray Price*. When I talk about artists who have moved on—Bob Wills and Ernest Tubb, Hank Williams and Johnny Cash, Ray Charles and Waylon Jennings, George Jones and Merle Haggard—I feel like I'm talking about souls that are still with us, souls that still live with us. That's 'cause their souls are in their music.

They say show business is about staying in fashion. I never believed that. That's talk made up by marketing men. Music men and music women know that good music never goes *out* of fashion. Like the sun, it rises every morning. Like the

moon, it lights up the night. Like the seasons, it keeps changing but stays rooted in the earth.

I guess that's why, eighty years after Sister and I started
playing music, we're still at it. When I go out there every
night and look over to my right, there she is. Bobbie Nelson.
Doing what she's always done with grace and style.

In addition to having a technical musical virtuosity I can't
match, Bobbie has something else I lack: a pure and forgiving
heart. I don't doubt the benefits of forgiveness. And I do my
best to forgive and forget. But I'm a lot better at forgetting
than forgiving.

Give you an example: Back in Abbott, when Bud Fletcher's folks took Bobbie's three young sons from her, she ultimately forgave them. Even today you'll never hear her say a
bad word about them. She hasn't just forgiven them in her
mind, she's actually forgiven them in her heart. You ask me
about those people and I won't mince words. Though they're
all long gone, I'm still going to say that they treated Sister like
dirt. I still get all worked up about it.

Jack Fletcher is another example. There's no excusing
how he acted when my nephew Michael got sick. In Jack's
mind, Michael was a pariah, an untouchable. At the very moment when my nephew needed the most support, Jack
treated him like a leper. That's a hard thing to forgive. In fact,
I don't know anyone capable of such forgiveness except my
sister.

SISTER

TOP: *Freddy and his mom, the Bahamas, 2019*
BOTTOM: *Ellee, Freddy, Bobbie, and Lisa in Austin, 2019*

After I lost my sons, I did a lot of reflection. I tried to be prayerful about every move I made. I don't mean I lived a perfect life. Far from it. But I knew the tragedies, coming so close together, could only be weathered if I found a wellspring of strength from deep inside. Willie keeping me in the band went a long way to provide that strength. I also derived strength from my ongoing friendship with Joel Mitchell. When Jack was going for all my money, Joel's legal brilliance protected me. In the years that followed, Joel and I became intimate again. And though the intimacy was satisfying, it was our friendship that brought the greatest pleasure. I did love Joel, but not with the romantic fervor that I loved Bud and Jack.

Bud and Jack, for all their shortcomings, were the two great loves of my life. That's why when they both fell ill, I felt compelled to support them. After Bud's car accident, I visited him at the VA Hospital in Dallas. And despite all that had transpired between me and Jack, we also reconciled before he passed a few years ago. That isn't to say we lived together again. That would never happen. But when I learned he'd contracted pneumonia, I went to see him. For the last three years of his life, I visited him often and brought him meals whenever I was off the road. I didn't tell anyone because I feared they would judge me for being too soft or too forgiving. When Jack was too sick to live alone, I drove him to a nursing home. As he became frailer, I stayed by his side. I still cherish his last words to me. "You're the one," he said.

As a child, playing revivals with Brother Dunson in small villages spread over Hill County, I remember playing "Let Go and Let God Have His Wonderful Way." *His wonderful way.* Those words stuck.

I believe God's wonderful way is to forgive. I can say today that I hold no ill toward anyone. I can also say that I feel forgiveness is almost a selfish act because it does so much good for those willing to forgive. The only other option is carrying anger and resentment, a heavy burden that weighs us down and makes us miserable.

I know full well that Bud did not do right by me. The same is true of Jack. I can go on and on about their faults. But I cannot lie and say those faults kept me from loving those two men. I loved them deeply. And because I forgave them, I feel free of whatever damages they did in the past.

In Jack's case, I was there during the moment of his death. I held his hand and prayed that his transition would be peaceful. My eyes filled with tears. Because of forgiveness, love was present.

I realize that I come from a different generation when women were more likely to turn over the power to men. I've been gratified to see how things have changed. I'm glad that women are standing up for themselves, claiming their equal rights and calling out men who bully, intimidate, and abuse them. All that is for the good. All that represents progress.

When I talk about forgiveness, I am not saying that women should tolerate abuse, mental or physical. It took me too long to remove myself from romantic relationships that had turned against me. But even if I had acted sooner, left Bud and Jack years before their behaviors had worsened, I still would have loved them. I can't explain it. But I do have to say it. I couldn't, and still can't, control the direction of my love. Love is mysterious and powerful. It goes where it goes. Sometimes it lands in dangerous territory. That's when wisdom is so important—being wise enough to realize that, in spite of the strength of the love, you may be risking your own well-being. At critical times in my life, I lacked that wisdom.

That's why in forgiving Bud and Jack, I now understand that I also have to forgive myself. I have to extend to myself the same compassion I extended to these men. I was not wise enough in the ways of romance. I was not worldly enough in the ways of finance. My default position is to blame myself for everything, but my own deficiencies require forgiveness. That isn't easy. But in prayerful moments, when my mind is clear and my heart is focused on the goodness of God, I feel that forgiveness. It may last but for a fleeting moment, but it's there.

Gratitude fuels forgiveness. If I live in gratitude, it's much easier to forgive. And I sincerely do feel grateful. I'm essentially a sideman—to use the old-school term—in a really good band. My job is to make sure my brother has the musical support he merits. I love that job. I'm grateful for that job. Grateful, for example, that he thinks well enough of me to haul a seven-foot Steinway grand piano wherever we go. I'm grateful that there's someone to tune that piano and grateful that my fingers are still nimble enough to hit the right keys.

I'm grateful that whatever befell me, I didn't lose my mind or my sense of morality. I'm grateful, too, for the pacemaker that has lengthened my life.

I'm grateful for the very concept of gratitude because without it I'd be lost. With it, I'm a happy woman. I've had great friendships, great love affairs, great musical experiences in concert halls, showrooms, and barrooms the world over.

The years I spent with my sons Randy and Michael still live in my heart and always will. I feel their spirit every day. My son Freddy has had a wonderful career. As a drummer, he played with artists like Guy Clark and Billy Joe Shaver before building a recording complex in the building that once housed the Austin Opry House, the old Willie Hilton. It warmed my heart when Freddy named the facility in honor of his father, Arlyn Bud Fletcher. I'm proud to say that Arlyn Studios has become one of the most successful recording operations in the country.

Bud would be so proud of him.

I am.

BROTHER

Bobbie on the tour bus, photographed by Ellee, 2018

Right now we're on the road again. We're always on the road again. I'm on the bus with my wife, Annie, and Sister Bobbie. In a few hours we'll be pulling into Bangor, Maine, for a big summer show. I'm not sure how many gigs we've played so far this year, but it's a whole bunch and we don't seem to be slowing down. By the time you'll be reading this, Bobbie will be pushing ninety and I'll be pushing eighty-eight.

I think back to the beginning. Different time. Different

world. But is it? Isn't Bobbie just a little girl who fell in love with the sound of an organ and a piano? Aren't I just a little boy who fell in love with the sound of a guitar? The girl grew up to become a woman. The boy became a man. They tripped and triumphed and suffered and survived. But the essentials never changed.

The girl loved music.

The boy loved music.

And music loved them.

Music provided and protected and still provides and protects them as the bus roars down the highway.

Soon the people will arrive at the show.

Soon the music will start.

ACKNOWLEDGMENTS

WILLIE

I would like to acknowledge and thank my parents Ira and Myrle, grandparents Alfred and Nancy, my wife Annie, all my children, and especially my sister Bobbie, who has taken this crazy ride with me all the way.

From Abbott, Texas, to the world stage, she has been at my side, and I wouldn't have wanted to do it without her.

I'd like to thank my manager Mark Rothbaum, Brian Greenbaum at CAA, my book agent David Vigliano, Ben Greenberg at Random House, and all my lawyers who have allowed me to walk free. My publicist Elaine Schock, David Ritz for being a great writer and so easy to work with. I'd like to acknowledge all the fans who have come out to see me, for generations, and allowed me to live this beautiful life. You think I give to you when you come to a show, but it's you who fill me with the energy you give.

I am grateful.

BOBBIE

I would like to thank Freddy Fletcher, Lisa Fletcher, Ellee Fletcher Durniak, Phyllis Fletcher, Mildred Wilcox, Lana Nelson, Mark Rothbaum, David Ritz, Ben Greenberg, and of course my beloved brother, Willie.

DAVID

I would like to thank Bobbie and Willie for trusting me with this precious project. And great gratitude to Mark Rothbaum, who came up with the idea for a sister-brother book, Freddy Fletcher, Ben Greenberg, David Vigliano, and Kaeli Subberwal.

ABOUT THE AUTHORS

WILLIE NELSON is an American country music singer-songwriter, as well as an author, poet, actor, and activist. He was inducted into the Country Music Hall of Fame in 1993.

BOBBIE NELSON is a pianist, singer, and member of the band Willie Nelson and Family.

DAVID RITZ has collaborated on books with everyone from Ray Charles to Aretha Franklin.

ABOUT THE TYPE

This book is set in Spectrum, a typeface designed in the 1940s and the last from the distinguished Dutch type designer Jan van Krimpen (1892–1958). Spectrum is a polished and reserved font.